GRACE, GOLD
& GLORY

GRACE, GOLD & GLORY
My Leap of Faith

GABRIELLE DOUGLAS

With Michelle Burford

ZONDERVAN®

ZONDERVAN.com/
AUTHORTRACKER
follow your favorite authors

ZONDERVAN

Grace, Gold & Glory
Copyright © 2012 by Gabrielle Douglas

This title is also available as a Zondervan ebook.
Visit *www.zondervan.com/ebooks*.

Requests for information should be addressed to:
Zondervan, *Grand Rapids, Michigan* 49530

ISBN 978-0-310-74061-2

Scripture quotations marked NASB are taken from the *New American Standard Bible*. Copyright © 1960, 1962, 1963, 1971, 1972, 1973, 1975, 1977, 1995 by The Lockman Foundation. Used by permission.

Scripture quotations marked NIV are taken from The Holy Bible, *New International Version®, NIV®*. Copyright © 1973, 1978, 1984, 2011 by Biblica, Inc.™ Used by permission. All rights reserved worldwide.

Scripture quotations marked NKJV are from the New King James Version. Copyright © 1982 by Thomas Nelson, Inc. Used by permission. All rights reserved.

Scripture quotation on page 202 taken from the Complete Jewish Bible (CJB). Copyright © 1998 by David H. Stein. All rights reserved.

Scripture quotations also taken from the King James Version.

Any Internet addresses (websites, blogs, etc.) and telephone numbers in this book are offered as a resource. They are not intended in any way to be or imply an endorsement by Zondervan, nor does Zondervan vouch for the content of these sites and numbers for the life of this book.

Cover design: Cindy Davis
Front cover photo: Neil Leifer/Getty Images
Poster photo: Al Tielemans/Getty Images
Back cover, spine, and flap photos: Kevin Jairaj/US PRESSWIRE; Julian Finney/ Getty Images; Brian Killian/WireImage/Getty Images
Interior design: Ben Fetterley and Greg Johnson/Textbook Perfect

Printed in the United States of America

12 13 14 15 16 17 18 /DCI/ 20 19 18 17 16 15 14 13 12 11 10 9 8 7 6 5 4 3 2 1

Dedication

To my mom:
*I couldn't have accomplished my dream without your
constant support, sacrifice, and belief in me.
I love you with all of my heart.*

To my sister Arielle:
*Since the day you convinced Mom to put me in
gymnastics, you've never stopped cheering for me.
I appreciate you so much.*

To my sister Joyelle:
*You have prayed for me endlessly and encouraged
me even more than that. My life just wouldn't
be the same without you in it.*

To my brother, Johnathan:
*You have always been and still are my best friend.
Thank you for refusing to let me stop fighting.*

Introduction

*January 2, 2012, in West Des Moines, Iowa — seven
months before the London Summer Olympics*

GYMNASTICS IS NOT MY PASSION ANYMORE. I'D DRAFTED THOSE WORDS
onto my smartphone as a text message two weeks before
my mother and two of my older siblings, Joyelle and
John, flew from Virginia Beach, Virginia, to celebrate
Christmas and my sixteenth birthday with me. In October
2010, I'd left my hometown and family and moved to
Iowa so I could be coached by elite trainer Liang Chow.
I'd been dreaming of an Olympic gold medal since I was
eight — but as I became more and more homesick, that
dream seemed like a zillion miles away. That's when I
knew I needed to have the toughest conversation of my
life: I had to tell Mom that I wanted to quit.

"Here we are," Mom announced as she rounded the
corner into the parking lot of Chow's gym. I was there
that afternoon for my usual training session at two

thirty—something even a family visit couldn't stop. Before either of us could get out of the silver Nissan Versa, I handed my phone to Mom. She lowered her eyes to the phone's screen and scanned the words that I'd been too scared to say out loud—which is why I had written them down:

> Gymnastics is not my passion anymore. I want to get famous off of running track, or I want to try dancing, or become a singer. I can get a job at Chick-Fil-A in Virginia Beach and live off the 14 grand I just won at World Championships. I just want to be a normal teenage kid. I am so homesick. I just want to come home.

As Mom read my letter in silence, her eyes narrowed and her expression turned to stone. "You're breaking my heart here, Brie," she said. I could feel my stomach flip as I hunched my shoulders and looked down at my lap. "You've been doing gymnastics for ten years, and now you want to run *track*? Have you lost your mind?"

I hadn't lost my mind—but I had definitely lost my fire. Did I understand the enormous sacrifices my mother had made just so I could become an elite gymnast? Absolutely. Had I been the one who begged Mom to send me to live with a host family in butt-freezing West Des Moines, Iowa, for nearly two years of rigorous training? Of course. But looking back on it, had I understood what it would actually feel like to live through the painful injuries and daily demands without my mom and siblings at my side every day? Not even sorta. It's one thing to keep fighting for your dream when you're surrounded by the four family members who know you the best. It's an entirely different thing to push toward that dream when you feel alone and totally homesick.

"I'm not trying to break your heart, Mom," I said.

"Look, you're going to go into this gym right now, and you're going to work out today," Mom said in a tone that told me a smackdown was on the way. "I've worked my behind off for you to be here because this is what you said you wanted—and I've loved helping you strive for your dream. But you're not going to repay me like this."

"But I'm not passionate—"

"That's a lie!" Mom cut in. "Just a couple months ago, you said you wanted to be the world champion. Is there something going on at the gym or with your host family that you're not telling me?" I shook my head from side to side. "Then you're gonna have to explain yourself to me—'cause this right here isn't making any sense."

I could feel teardrops forming on my lower lids as I pressed my palms into the seat. "I just don't want to do it anymore," I finally said.

"Well, that choice is not yours to make," Mom snapped. "You've got your coaches, Chow and Li, involved in this dream. They've put everything they have into your coaching! You've got your host family, Travis and Missy, involved in this dream. They've opened up their home and turned their lives upside down to accommodate your training schedule! You've got hundreds of people rallied around, helping you to get to the next level."

"But, Mom," I cut in, my lower lip suddenly trembling, "you don't know how it feels!"

Mom paused and looked directly at me. "I know you miss home, Brie," she said, her tone softening just a little before she shifted right into the next gear. "But you've signed a contract that says you will represent your country to the best of your ability. You've got a responsibility to your teammates. And now you just want to walk away? I will not let you be dishonorable. If gymnastics is not your passion, then at the very least, you will finish the season. I didn't raise you and your brother and sisters to be quitters."

"It's my body and my choice," I said stiffly, staring straight ahead at the dashboard. "And I'm not going to do it."

Without a word, Mom turned the key in the ignition, sped through the parking lot, and swerved left onto the main road that leads to the gym. And if you think she was upset before—this is when she really lost it.

"I can't believe you're doing this!" she shouted, slamming her wrists against the steering wheel to the beat of each one of her words. As the car's tires wavered from left to right, Mom hit her brakes just in time for us to miss a pole on the right-hand side of the road. She then pulled over for part two. "All the people who've said you can't do this, the people who've doubted that your dream could ever come true—I guess you're just going to let them win," Mom said. Her eyes filled with tears. "Why didn't you just tell me a long time ago that you wanted to quit? What a waste—a total waste."

"I love you, Mom," I whispered in an attempt to calm her down. I reached over and began rubbing her back. Yes, I still wanted to quit gymnastics—and PS, I also wanted to make this argument long enough for me to miss that day's training session with Coach Chow—but I thought coughing up a little affection might keep me alive a few minutes longer.

"No, you don't love me!" Mom shot back. I knew she didn't mean those words—and she knew it too—but the tension of the moment brought out so many emotions. "You can pack your bags and buy yourself a plane ticket back to Virginia Beach," she told me. "But when you get there, you'd better go live with your grandmother— because you're not moving back in with me."

Everyone around me knows that I've always had just one hero—my mom. But on the very first Monday of 2012, I couldn't have been more mad at her. In fact, after my mother, my sister Joyelle, and my brother, John, flew home to Virginia the next morning, I was still so furious that I didn't Skype with Mom for two weeks. I knew she was right. I was just way too upset to admit it.

The next afternoon as I dragged myself into Chow's gym for a hard workout, Mom's words were still fresh in my head. I thought of the hundreds of double shifts she'd worked in order to pay for my training. I thought of my two sisters: Arielle, who gave up ballroom dancing, and Joyelle, who stopped ice skating so that our single mom could afford to keep me in gymnastics. I thought of my father—the one person who'd missed out on so much of the dream I was about to set aside. I thought of my closest friend and my only brother, John—the one whose little pep talk turned out to be the big miracle that changed everything that month. But I'll come back to that part.

For now, here's what you need to know: Exactly 210 days before I ever attempted my first vault in the London Summer Olympics, my leap of faith came *this close* to ending in a crash of disaster. That's why this isn't simply the story of how a one-handed cartwheel at age three eventually landed me on the top of an Olympic podium. It's also the story of how the people who love me the most literally lifted me up during the lowest moments of my journey. It's the story of how I finally faced the truth about a dad I hardly even know. It's a testimony of the one huge lesson that I'm still learning every day: With strong faith in God and some serious determination, every dream is possible—especially if your mama refuses to let you fly home, fry chicken, and give up.

My Father

In one way, I know my dad. In another way, I never have. He was there. He was gone. He was suddenly back again. Strangely, the truth lives in every one of these statements, as well as in the cracks between them. While I can't tell you all there is to know about this man who gave me life, I can tell you this: The story of my dream to make it to the Olympics has both everything and nothing to do with him. That's why I'm finally choosing to share it.

My first memories of my father are dim—just faded images of him picking me up or playing with me when I was a toddler. In later years, my recollections are more concrete. Living briefly with him and his parents in Chesapeake, Virginia. Looking on in silence as he and my mother separated. Overhearing my mother implore Dad to spend time with me and my siblings. Going fishing with him before I moved to Iowa. In the chapters to follow, you'll read about the countless joys, stresses, tumbles, and thrills that line my path to London. Alongside that account, you'll experience my dad in the same way that I did as a girl—in a series of brief snapshots and scenes that led me toward a place I'm still trying to reach.

I have always loved my father. I just haven't always understood him. Maybe gathering up the pieces of what I remember about our moments together will somehow reveal him more clearly to me. That is the only real reason to reflect. That is also my deepest prayer.

Chapter One

By His stripes we are healed.
—ISAIAH 53:5, NKJV

MY MOTHER ALMOST DIED ON THE DAY SHE HAD ME: DECEMBER 31, 1995. As Mom gripped the arm rails of her hospital bed in Newport News, Virginia, a doctor and nurse tripped over themselves trying to stop her from bleeding to death. No one could figure out exactly why she was hemorrhaging so badly, but they finally gave Mom a series of medications that made her blood clot. An hour later, a nurse bundled me up and placed my six-pound, five-ounce body in Mom's arms—that warm spot I've returned to a thousand times since.

Back then, cash was tight. Very tight. I'm the baby in my family, and that made me the last of four mouths to feed. Since three of those mouths arrived back to back (Mom was prego every year between 1993 and 1995, and each birth came with major complications), my mother had to be on bed rest. So Mom let go of her job as a bank teller, a position that only paid about $20,000 a year; and my father, who worked on and off at various jobs, wasn't bringing in much money. That's why my mother and father loaded up a U-Haul trailer and moved us all to Oklahoma so we could find a fresh start.

Mom had once dreamed of becoming a lawyer. But after she had Arielle in 1989, she set aside college at Norfolk State University in order to keep food on the table. A couple years later, when she was twenty-one, she met my father and they got married. As they considered a move from Virginia to Tulsa, Oklahoma, after I was born, the plan was for my mother to go to Bible school and for my dad—who already had a background in ministry—to continue his training. At the time, my parents were both part of a movement called Word of Faith, a set of teachings that involves claiming and standing by God's promises in the Bible. So Tulsa—a city filled with Word of Faith mega-churches and Bible schools—was the perfect spot.

When we rolled into Tulsa in February 1996, my family drove right into one of the worst situations we've ever survived. My mother and father had scrounged up a thousand or so bucks to cover the deposit and rent on an apartment, but because of a miscommunication between my parents and the owner, that place fell through. So rather than sinking all their money into a hotel, my parents first looked around for apartment vacancies. When they couldn't find a single rental that was in their budget, we ended up living in the only place that wouldn't cost them a cent—the floor of our blue Dodge van.

So that's how we became homeless—as in parked in a dark, damp, and rundown lot for several months. Why didn't they reach out to their families for help? Because Mom was sick and tired of asking her own parents to lend us money, so she just wanted to stick it out this time. When my mother called her mom from a pay phone—not many cell phones back then!—my grandmother kept asking, "What's your address?"

"I felt humiliated," Mom once told me when I asked her about the experience. "We removed a bucket seat from the back of the van so that we'd all have more space to lie down, huddle together, and try to sleep at night." After lifting me up to her breast to feed me, Mom would rock me in her arms. Later, after my mother had patted me on my back till I was asleep, she'd carefully spread a napkin on the floor to prepare the only daily meal our family could afford—peanut butter and jelly sandwiches. "And since we'd gotten to Tulsa right in the middle of winter," Mom recalls, "it felt like it was below freezing some nights."

Just to keep us warm, Mom dressed my sisters and brother in every shirt, pants, underwear, and socks she could find. With all those layers, my siblings must have looked like little stuffed animals! My sister Arielle was already six at the time, so Mom enrolled her in school by using the address of a post-office box. In between shuttling Arielle back and forth to first grade with the few drops of gas we had in our van, Mom practiced the alphabet with Joyelle, who was two, and John, who was one. For hours, our mother would entertain them with stories or let them color while my father, who worked sporadically as a day laborer, was away from the van. At just two and a half months old, I lay there next to all of them, wrapped in every blanket Mom could find.

That April, my parents' tax refund check showed up in their temporary PO Box—and that gave us enough money to move into a small room in a Super 8 hotel. But after two months of shelling out $50 a night, they'd blown through every dime of their money. In place of cash, my parents began making promises to the hotel manager that they would pay up soon—and that worked until their bill climbed to more than $300. So one afternoon when we were away from the hotel, the manager evicted us from our room and removed our few belongings. In fact, just to get our suitcases back, my grandmother had to wire some money—by this time, Mom had 'fessed up to her parents that she and Dad were flat broke. Once that money ran out, we stayed for three weeks with a newlywed couple my parents had met through a local ministry. But after awhile, we ended up back where we began—crowded together in the back of a Dodge. We spent most of our five months in Tulsa living on that hard floor.

By spring, I was a few months old—and getting smaller by the day. (I've always been tiny—don't rub it in!) Because my weight kept dropping, my parents became concerned. In fact, my mother told me that a couple of people accused her of starving me. She fed me constantly, but I threw up everything. At one point, Mom says it felt like I only weighed about four or five pounds. I'd received one round of vaccinations at birth, but because my family had no insurance, Mom hadn't taken me back to the doctor. Mom eventually received a letter from the hospital where I was born—a friend back in Virginia had forwarded the note to our PO Box. Doctors had gotten the results of the blood test they run on all newborns. They'd diagnosed me with a life-threatening disease called Branched Chain Ketoaciduria. Sounds scary, right? Basically, it's a rare blood disorder found in infants who can't process particular kinds of protein. The condition is also known as maple syrup urine disease (MSUD)—mostly because it makes a baby's pee smell just like a stack of molasses-soaked pancakes. Maybe that explains why I've always loved me some IHOP.

But all jokes aside, I was sick. Seriously sick. And in addition to the blood disease, Mom was also pretty sure I had whooping cough, because I sounded like a child she'd heard on a public service announcement on television. "I was afraid for your life," Mom recently told me. "Because we had no money and no health insurance, I was afraid to take you to the doctor. I just didn't know what to do, so I leaned on my faith." Mom prayed for me every single day as she quoted (and requoted!) a powerful Scripture, Isaiah 53:5: "But He was wounded for our transgressions, He was bruised for our iniquities; the chastisement of our peace was upon Him, and by His stripes we are healed." As it turns out, God answered Mom's prayers and came through with a miracle: By the time I was six months old, the disease had gone away. Completely. And to this day, I am healthy—even if I am only 4'11" and 94 pounds.

By the summer of 1996, my parents were so over the whole Tulsa thing—so our next stop was Texas. We moved into the two-bedroom apartment of Mom's Uncle Ben and Aunt Teresa in Irving. My uncle offered my dad job leads, and Dad eventually began working at a used car dealership; but because he didn't sell many cars, he didn't earn much money. So he quit that job. Around that time, Mom's aunt and uncle traveled to the Olympic Games in Atlanta. Years later, Mom told me that her uncle left a note with her. "In that letter, my uncle wrote that he loved me and my kids, and that we were always welcome to stay with him," Mom recalls. "He also wrote that he wouldn't support a grown man, so we had to be moved out by the time they returned from the Olympics." Arielle told me that Mom began looking for work too, since my father wasn't working. It didn't take long for Mom to land a job in the collections department at Citibank. In addition, Mom's friend—the same one who'd once forwarded the hospital's note about my blood disease—knew a young couple in Dallas. That friend asked the couple if they'd be willing to take us in temporarily, and they agreed. In the fall of 1996, Mom had saved up enough money for us to move into our own apartment in Richardson, Texas.

Later that year when Mom celebrated my first birthday, I'd already been given the nickname my whole family still calls me: Brie Baby. Since then, we've put every possible spin on that name, including Brie Cheese and

Breezy. And then there's my personal favorite—Easy, Breezy, Beautiful Cover Girl. But if you ask me, none of those nicknames roll off the tongue quite as gracefully as my full name does: Gabrielle, which means "God's able-bodied one." When that blood disease almost snatched away my life, it might've seemed that I wouldn't really live up to my name. But my heavenly Father had something totally different in mind. In Texas, as I grew stronger by the month—and as my mother worked to turn our family's financial crisis into a comeback—my name's meaning became a sneak preview of all that would come next.

Chapter Two

*It is God who is at work in you, both to will
and to work for His good pleasure.*
—PHILIPPIANS 2:13, NASB

"GET DOWN FROM THERE, BRIE!" MOM SHOUTED IN THE DIRECTION OF my crib. I'd gripped all ten of my fingers around the wooden bars and was attempting to inch my entire body up toward the top of the crib. Just in time to keep me from falling, Mom darted over to the crib's edge and pulled me into her arms. "You're going to hurt yourself, child!"

I wasn't even quite two—yet I'd already turned my bed and our entire Richardson apartment into my own little obstacle course. With my days as a fragile, sickly baby long behind me, I'd grown into a teeny tot with the strongest grip my parents had ever witnessed in a child of my age. And I was a toughie: Even when I dove off the furniture and bumped my head, Mom says I would simply sit up, look around, let out one of my trademark giggles, and then keep right on jumping and wiggling. My older brother, John, and I are only fourteen months apart—so every time he attempted a hop or tumble in our living room, I was right there behind him with a copycat move. And that was just the beginning. Month after month, my daredevil attempts expanded to include everything from scaling to the top of a closet door ("Look, Mom!" I yelled from up above) to leaping off the back of our sofa and onto the kitchen table (I was pretending I was Supergirl). As it turns out, I can flip far better than I can fly—I hit my chin on the table's edge and blood came spouting out. Ouch!

John and I have been practically inseparable since we were tots. Even way back then, he was the protective older brother. Mom told me that once when I was two and John was three, I rode around a playground in a toy car—until a little boy came over and pushed me out of my seat. When John saw that, he ran up to the boy, pushed him out of the car and then pulled me back into the seat. He was like, "Go ahead, Brie. You can ride." So even when we were tiny, he was on my side. Though we've both grown much taller since then, not much else has changed between us.

Unless you've been vacationing on Saturn, you've probably heard that my oldest sister, Arielle, a former gymnast, showed me how to do a perfect cartwheel when I was just three and she was just nine. The two of us also practiced all kinds of other skills, aka tricks: spider-walk handstands, the splits, bridges, and back walkovers. "You were so flexible!" Arielle recently reminded me. "And you learned everything super fast. Pretty soon, you'd gone over my head—you'd already excelled my level of expertise!" In fact, after a week of mirroring Arielle's moves, I went solo: I taught myself how to do a cartwheel on one hand. That's when my sister really noticed that I had a special gift.

"Mom, you need to put her in gymnastics!" Arielle hounded. Our mother's answer was always the same: not enough dough. Plus, Arielle once broke her wrist in two places while doing a back handspring in her bedroom, which is why my mother took her out of classes for a few years. Mom didn't want to risk the same kind of injury with her youngest child—her baby girl.

"But she's so talented," Arielle pleaded. "Why don't you put her in?"

"I'm not interested," Mom answered flatly.

This exact negotiation went down time and time again in 1998. Then in 1999. Then in 2000, which is the year my parents separated and we headed to Virginia.

At first, we all moved into the two-bedroom house of my mother's mom, Miss Carolyn. Arielle first began calling my grandmother by that name back in 1990, after my grandmother married her now ex-husband, Marcus. Marcus's little girl didn't know what to call my grandmother, so she dubbed her "Miss Carolyn." Arielle overheard the name and followed suit. When Joyelle, John, and I came along, we copied Arielle. When we arrived in 2000, we turned the downstairs of Miss Carolyn's house into a kids' bedroom. Arie and Joy slept on the couch, and John and I took the pullout futon bed. When Mom's younger sister, Bianca (my aunt!) came home from college in the summer of 2001, Bianca reclaimed her bedroom—and Mom went to stay with a friend.

Starting in November 2001, our family became separated. For about nine months, John, Joyelle, and I lived with my father, who had moved back from Texas after we did, and his parents at my grandparents' home in Chesapeake, Virginia; Arielle stayed with Miss Carolyn in Virginia Beach, while Mom stayed with her friend. This gave our mother the chance to work around the clock and get back on her financial feet. We missed living with our mother, but we kept ourselves plenty busy around my grandparents' neighborhood.

That year, I got my first bike. John, Joyelle, and I rolled through my grandparents' neighborhood—only their bikes were two-wheelers, while I still had training wheels! Do you know how annoying it is to ride a bike made for babies? I so wanted to balance on a regular bike. Whenever they sped up, they could just leave me in the dust. "Hey, wait a minute," Joy pointed out one day, "your training wheels aren't even *on* correctly." So for at least a couple days, I'd been pouting for no good reason—my trainers hadn't even been touching the ground! Without even knowing it, I'd taught myself how to ride a two-wheeler. Joy and John were pretty impressed, and I was just happy to be rolling with the big kids!

Around the neighborhood, the three of us made new friends. Billy and David were our two best pals, and they lived across the street from us. We'd all play hide and seek and freeze tag, and for the longest time, I had a major crush on Billy. He was so tall! We all hung out together for hours every day; then at nightfall, we'd catch fireflies or play one last round of cops and robbers on our bikes.

By 2002, Mom had squirreled away enough money to buy a three-bedroom, 1,378-square-foot town house. How awesome it was to have our whole family under one roof again! It didn't take long for Arielle to reboot her campaign: "Mom," she begged, "you need to put Brie in gymnastics."

Though Mom had a couple extra dollars to her name by this point, she still had no intention of signing me up for classes. She probably only did so because she needed a long nap. But here's the official reason Mom still gives me: "I was afraid you were going to hurt yourself!" she says. "I figured I should get you some formal instruction so you could burn off some of that energy." That's just how much of a spark plug I'd become.

Mom intended to raise a gymnastics star — only I wasn't the star she had in mind. Back when Mom had put then–three-year-old Arielle in classes, my older sister had been so focused and talented that Mom was sure she'd become an elite gymnast one day. And if there'd been enough money to go around, Arielle might've been the one to mount those uneven bars in London. "Arielle was on her way to becoming a phenomenal gymnast," Mom recalls. "I just wish I had enough money to take her all the way." Now can you see why I always give so much credit to my big sister? Even though she didn't get to pursue her original passion, Arielle was one of my loudest cheerers in the stands when I represented the USA in the 2012 Olympics. But that's getting way ahead of the story.

Let's circle back to the fall day in October 2002 that Mom loaded us into her car and drove us down to Gymstrada, a local training center that offers recreational gym classes. In October 2000, when we returned to Virginia, Mom had found a job in the recovery department at Household International (now HSBC), so she had enough extra cash to even consider handing over money for classes. Mom initially signed up all four of us for gymnastics lessons—the idea was to keep us in one spot!—but that didn't quite work out. Arielle had a passion for gymnastics, of course, but by this time, she was already thirteen—and she felt she was too old to start a serious competitive gymnastics career. So Arielle took a tumbling class and used the skills she learned to rock her moves as a competitive cheerleader on the squad of American Cheer Elite (ACE). Later, Mom let her follow her coaches from ACE when they started another competitive squad called Fame All Stars. Joyelle didn't like doing gymnastics at all and decided to try ice skating; she absolutely loved it and excelled quickly. John enjoyed the tumbling at Gymstrada; he just didn't want to be a male gymnast. Instead, he wanted to spend his time on the field playing tag football with the neighborhood recreation league. And me? Well, the day I stepped through the front doors of Gymstrada as a six-year-old, I instantly knew what I still know to this day: I was in exactly the right place.

"Come back here, Brie!" Mom called out as I dashed onto the gym floor and did over splits. I was a real show-off back then. Before the handful of other students had even gathered, I leapt around that gym in my (cute!) blue leotard (nicknamed a leo) and did every single trick I'd learned from Arielle. "You need to stay put until class begins," Mom warned, but I was way too excited to wait. At home, I did all my flipping and tumbling in a small space, so you can imagine how I felt when I walked into Gymstrada — an enormous room with lots of beams, bars, and trampolines for me to play on. In retrospect, the gym really wasn't all that big — but when you're six, everything seems gigantic. When I finished the trial class that day, I had just one question for Mom: "Do I get to come back?" The answer was yes — and a lot more frequently than even Mom had anticipated.

"Is this your daughter?" Gymstrada's owner asked my mom after my first session. He tilted his head in my direction, and Mom nodded yes. "How much gymnastics training has she had?" My mother paused, then formed the number zero with her right fist, which she put up to her right eye. "Are you kidding me?" he said, furrowing his brow. "Your daughter has too much raw talent for just a Saturday recreational class." So that afternoon, Mom signed me up for a different schedule — gymnastics lessons every Tuesday, Thursday, and Saturday for a total of six hours each week.

That same fall, the owner launched a pilot program called TOPs — that's short for Talent Opportunity

Program. TOPs is affiliated with USA Gymnastics (USAG), the organization that oversees gymnastics in America. So when you participate in TOPs, that automatically puts you on the radar of USAG's national staff. And if a young gymnast has her heart set on competing in the Olympics one day—wink, wink!—having the TOPs connection can be very beneficial. Though I had no clue what earning a gold medal was all about (at that age, I just wanted to jump around), I still took my spot in TOPs.

I don't believe in coincidence. So when I look back on all the experiences that led to my first day at Gymstrada, I can definitely see how the Lord put me on the path that He designed for me. Who could've predicted that I'd go from being a scrawny baby on the floor of a Dodge van to being the bounciest kid in my family? And besides that, who knew that having ants in my pants would prompt Mom to enroll me in gymnastics? Oh, that's right—God knew. He still always does.

The Safe Spot

I don't recall much about my parents' divorce—the first time they split, I was only four. After Mom and us kids returned to Virginia from Texas, Dad eventually came back there too.

For several months, John, Joyelle, and I lived with my father at his parents' home in Chesapeake. Dad's father owned a small neighborhood restaurant. Sometimes, our whole family would go there to have dinner together. "Come sit right here, baby," Dad would say. Each time I climbed up into my father's lap, I felt safe and loved.

Our dad quoted a lot of Scripture. "Death and life are in the power of the tongue," we'd sometimes hear him recite. Other times, he'd say things like, "Satan is just trying to get to me." My dad's father was a minister, and though my grandfather hadn't yet pastored a church of his own at that time, he encouraged my dad to go to Bible school and get into ministry. Dad followed that path. Once he finished high school in 1984, my father went to Bible school for three years. He graduated and then enlisted in the Virginia Air National Guard Reserves Unit. About six years later, in the fall of 1990, he and my mother met at Rock Church International in Virginia Beach. They dated for eight months before they exchanged their vows.

In my young eyes, my dad was everything a father should be. He was a Christian. He was a gentleman. He was handsome. And as far as I could tell, he could fix just about anything around the house — from a leaky faucet to a crack in the floor or wall. "Dad," I once told him, "I want to marry a guy just like you when I grow up." My father looked at me, smiled, and then reached down to pull me up into his broad arms.

Chapter Three

But store up for yourselves treasures in heaven.
—MATTHEW 6:20, NIV

I CAN STILL REMEMBER THE WAY THEY SPARKLED: TWO TINY, PERFECTLY rounded quarter-carat diamond earrings. In 2002, when I was almost seven, Mom surprised me with the earrings for Christmas—the first Christmas that she'd had enough money to purchase one special gift for each of her children. When I cracked open the lid of the black velvety box, the earrings stared back at me like a pair of glistening eyes. I cherished those diamond studs even more than I did my favorite gym leo—and that's saying a lot.

"Brie, can I wear your earrings today?" one of my sisters asked me one morning before school. (I won't be a snitch and tell you which sister it was, but here's a small hint: the first part of her name rhymes with *toy*.) "Absolutely not," I said as I tied up my shoes and marched out of the room we shared.

I thought that was the last of it—until I got to school

and noticed my sister actually *wearing* my most prized possession. That morning after I'd left the room, she'd sneaked into my jewelry box and taken my diamonds. When I caught her flashing them, she began pleading with me to let her keep them on during recess.

"Forget it," I said.

"But I promise I'll take very good care of them," she said in a voice that softened my heart a little.

"Okay," I reluctantly agreed. "Let's pinky promise on that." We lifted our pinky fingers and wrapped them around one another. Done deal. We then went off to our own classes until recess—which is when the drama really unfolded.

"Where's the other earring?" I'd just spotted my sister skipping back from the playground toward her classroom—and her left ear was diamondless. "Huh?" she said. She reached up to grab her earlobe, and her eyes widened at the realization that the earring was indeed missing. "I'm so sorry, Brie!" she shrieked. "I must've lost it during recess." I felt my heartbeat speed up as I glared at my sister. "This is the last time you'll ever borrow my stuff!" I shouted. As she slumped back to her class, I raced onto the playground. I was going to find that diamond.

For the next hour, instead of playing with the other kids in my class, I dug through every handful of dirt on that playground. As I crouched down on my knees and dragged my fingers through the brown mulch, hot tears slid from my lids and crashed onto the earth underneath me. "Where is it?" I repeated to myself as I dug. "It has to be here!"

But it wasn't.

And a few hours later, when I left school and went to Gymstrada for my training session, I was still completely heartbroken about those earrings. Do you know how much I adored those diamonds? As much as some women love their purses and some men love their cars. And if you multiply that love by two, you'll have some idea of what I was feeling. In a word, furious.

"How are you today?" my coach asked when I arrived at the gym. "Okay," I mumbled. I wasn't exactly okay, of course. But when you're a serious gymnast in training mode, you learn one thing pretty early: You have to set everything else aside and focus. One hundred percent. Even when you're a first grader who just parted with some major bling. That's why I simply slid into the splits that afternoon, prayed for a little extra strength, and did my very best to hold back more tears. And as surprising as it may sound, I already loved the sport so much that it cheered me up. I rarely wanted to miss a day of training— even if I was sick. Once, when I had a temperature of 103 degrees, the coach was like, "You need to go home, Gabrielle." After my mother picked me up, I said, "I'm gonna get behind!" Thank goodness I had a mom who insisted that I stay healthy—because all I knew is that I wanted to master my back layout step-out.

In those days, here's how my schedule went: school from eight in the morning to three in the afternoon. Car ride from school to Gymstrada between three and three thirty with tons of traffic along the way. A quickie snack (usually apples and bananas or crackers and cheese), followed by as much homework as I could squeeze in while in the backseat of Mom's white Nissan Altima. And then, of course, gym from four to eight every Tuesday and Thursday afternoon and from eight to noon every Saturday morning during my first year in TOPs.

In that first gymnastics season (btw, the season ran from fall to spring in Region 7, which was my region), I didn't actually learn many tricks. Since the other girls and I were so young, the coaches thought it was best to build our strength and flexibility by doing a lot of conditioning exercises. That way, once all the tumbling and flipping began, our bodies would be prepared for the action. In my case, that action got started in May 2003, the month I began training to compete at Level 4 in the Junior Olympics (JO) gymnastics program. You have to be at least six years old to compete at a Level 4. I was already seven.

The JO program has a range of levels—from 1 to 10. Many gyms around the country, including Gymstrada, start at a Level 4, which is the competitive level. Every gymnast works through the levels at his or her own pace. And how do you move up to the next level of difficulty? By earning a minimum score during a competition. You can't skip over any levels, but you can do more than one level in a year, at least in women's artistic gymnastics. Once you flip your way through all ten of the JO levels, you can then go on to train at the pre-elite and elite levels. And here's one last thing to keep straight in your head: JO and TOPs are two different programs. I started out only in TOPs, but by spring 2003, I was doing TOPs and JO at the same time. In other words, I wasn't exactly sitting around.

"Let's go, girls!" my coach called out to me and the other gymnasts one spring afternoon in 2003. About ten of us had gathered for our four-hour training. When you spend as much time together in the gym as we all did, you quickly become close; even our parents spent a lot of time together. To this day, some of the girls I met at Gymstrada—Cassie, Jasmine, Rebecca, and Julia—are still my friends, even though I don't get the chance to talk to them as much these days.

Before the start of class, I'd been catching up with one of my very best friends in that group—Kaiya Putman, my giggling buddy back then. Though we were in different groups, we were both Level 4 gymnasts, and we quickly became close. Kaiya's parents, Robert and Kim, also became good friends with my mom.

That day's session began the way most of them did: with our coach handing us a sheet that listed a series of exercises we needed to race through. And what was on that list? Handsprings on the floor; a mount on the beam for an exercise called a scale, which means balancing on one leg while holding the other leg higher than the hip.

All that was followed by connecting our beam skills (like scales, leaps, dances, and dismounts) into a complete routine; practicing our uneven bar skills; and then just a couple vaults. And last, if you learned all your skills, you got a treat: a few minutes of play time on the trampoline. "Bet you can't do *this*!" Kaiya and I would tease each other before attempting a trick on one of the apparatuses. Then if one of us performed an exercise that really impressed the coach, we'd tease each other: "You're just trying to show off!" We were kidding, of course — but only sorta.

When I wasn't at the gym, I was in school. After my family moved back to Virginia in 2000, Mom enrolled me in pre-K at Greenhill Farms Christian Academy, a private school where many professional people sent their children; Mom enrolled Joy and John there too. Like most parents, Mom did her best to give us a great education — but once she paid the rent and electric bill, she just didn't have much money to pay for that education. So, thankfully, she qualified for a program that covered half of the tuition for me and my siblings. I spent pre-K and kindergarten at Greenhill Farms in Norfolk before I moved on to first grade at Holland Elementary — the public school where my sister lost my precious you-know-whats. Mom wanted to keep us at Greenhill Farms, but once we moved into our town house near Scarborough Square in 2002, the campus was much too far away.

I loved school from the beginning. Even in pre-K and kindergarten at Greenhill Farms, Mom says I could spell huge words like *loquacious*. What was true at the gym was true in the classroom: I caught onto things very fast, and I often had energy left over to jump around once I was done. "Where's Bali?" a teacher once quizzed me as we looked at a map. Without hesitation, I pointed to the precise location: "It's right here," I announced. As Mom stood by with that "I'm so proud!" look on her face, my teacher challenged me with more and more difficult questions. It always felt awesome to get an answer right.

History is still my favorite subject. In particular, I loved reading about Dr. Martin Luther King, Jr. — and not just 'cause he was black, lol. Can you imagine how much nerve it takes to stand up for what you believe in, even when other people are threatening your life? Dr. King didn't have to imagine it; he *lived* it. And in 1963, when he took his place on the steps of the Lincoln Memorial and delivered his famous "I have a dream" speech, he did far more than just inspire a nation. He helped turn the world into a place where all of us could dream a little bigger.

In a way, my school time was also my gym time — the tricks never stopped! "Can you do a back flip?" one of my classmates asked me when I was in first grade. "Sure!" I answered before arching my back and lowering my palms to the floor. Over several months, I performed just about every skill I knew — for a price. Then one day Mom noticed my pockets loaded down with quarters, nickels, and dimes and she asked, "Brie, where did you get all this money?" I was like, "When I do tricks for the other kids, they give me their lunch money." Mom, of course, put an end to that.

Back then, I was a tomboy. Seriously. You'd think that a girl who tore up the playground just to find a diamond earring would be a total girlie girl—but that phase came (much!) later. At seven, my closest companion was my brother, John. He still is. And like John, I wore sweatpants all the time. Because I was always at the gym, I wore my hair back in a ponytail. Once when John and I were playing tag with a group of his friends, he and the other boys all took off their shirts—so I took off mine too. My mom and sisters were like, "Brie, put your shirt back on—you are not a boy." Sooo embarrassing!

On Sundays, just about everything came to a halt—no gym, no school, no tag in the backyard. My family went to Rock Church International, a nondenominational congregation in Virginia Beach. We didn't go every Sunday; sometimes we just stayed home and rested. But when we went, I loved learning about Jesus. (Plus, we got lollipops.) The only hard part was having to leave the side of my big brother; the classes were separated by age, so John and I were in two classes. I know this might be hard to believe now, but I was shy when I was a little girl. I'd actually cry real tears when John and I had to split up—and I still do, lol!

God's grace—that's something I heard a lot about at church and at home. Grace is all about receiving a gift you did nothing to earn and then passing that gift on to your family, friends, neighbors, and even strangers. Let's keep it real: I didn't really understand this whole idea when I was seven. But I now know that grace is the greatest treasure in the universe. If God can love us and forgive us unconditionally, how can we actually hold grudges against other people? I know, I know—at times, it's really a drag to hand out grace. But that's what I'm learning to do—even when a certain family member loses my all-time-favorite Christmas gift. Dang it, Joyelle!

The Disappearance

After we moved out of my father's parents' home in Chesapeake in 2001, I don't recall seeing my father hardly at all. Every now and then, I'd talk to him on the phone.

"How are you?" he'd ask, as if we'd just been with each other the day before.

"Fine," I'd say. "Where are you, Dad?"

"I'm training," he usually answered. But that always confused me, because he wasn't in the military full time.

In 2003, when I was eight, my father was deployed for eight months to Qatar, a small country in the Middle East. As a member of the reserves unit, he was required to serve a minimum of one week-end per month, along with two weeks of active-duty service each year. Three times during my childhood, he had to complete assignments overseas. Each of his deployments lasted for eight months; from 2008 to 2010, he also served on a temporary active duty assignment on a base in Norfolk, but though he was close by, I still didn't see him much.

"Where's Dad?" I asked Mom when Dad was supposed to be home from his duties abroad.

"He's on the military base," Mom often said, trying to protect me from what I was starting to suspect. At least for that moment, her vague answer was enough to satisfy my question — mostly because I wanted so badly to believe that Dad longed to be connected to us. But as weeks of silence turned into months, I was confused: *If Dad is back in Virginia, why doesn't he come around more often?* I dreamed of showing my father some of the same tricks I performed for the kids at school. I imagined what it would feel like to have him come to all my meets and cheer me on from the sidelines. The truth is that I missed my father — a lot.

Chapter Four

I can do all things through Christ
who strengthens me.
—PHILIPPIANS 4:13, NKJV

IT'S CALLED A KIP, AND IT'S ONE OF THE TOUGHEST SKILLS A GYMNAST first learns on the uneven bars. The kip begins with pulling yourself up to the low bar in a swing glide, bringing your toes to the bar, hoisting your hips up, and finally holding your whole upper body above the bar. The skill, which can be used to either mount the bar or connect elements in a routine, is a big part of just about every level of competition. That makes it a must-do skill. And in May 2003, I was failing at it. Big time.

"Put some power into that glide!" my Gymstrada coach, Dana, called out as I struggled to bring my toes up to the bar. Since spring, I'd been practicing all of my Level 4 skills—like the jump to handstand on the vault, the pullover on the bars, and the tuck jump on the beam. None of these tricks is a cinch, but at least I was making steady progress on each of them. Not so with the kip. I'd been trying to master it for nearly a year.

By June 2003, I'd messed up my kip so many times that I'd lost count. "Whoever gets the kip first wins a trophy," the coach told my group one afternoon. I wanted that trophy so badly that I could already visualize it standing proudly on a shelf in my bedroom. Each time I took my turn at the bar, I'd sway my body forward, and then *gliiiiiiiiiiiiiiiide*—right down onto the mat beneath the bars. Shoot—I was so close!

In early 2003, my training time doubled from six hours a week to about twelve. That's because Level 4 is the level that separates recreational gymnasts from those who are training for serious team competition. In the upcoming fall season, I was preparing to compete at what's called a compulsory level. What does that mean? It means that in Levels 4 to 6, every gymnast around the country performs the exact same routine at her level on each of the four apparatuses (vault, bars, beam, floor—and, yes, it always goes in that order, even at the Olympics).

Home was the one place where I could forget all about the crazy kip—and anything else that got on my nerves. On the weekends, John, Joyelle, and I would climb up into my mother's linen closet and pull down a pile of bed sheets so we could set up for our favorite activity—making a tent in the living room. We'd use the sofa pillows to hold up the tent's "walls" (the flat sheets) and then leave just enough of an opening at the front for all three of us to scoot in and camp out overnight.

"Wanna hear a scary story?" John would ask us, even though we all already knew the answer. After Joy and I had been terrified spitless by my brother's tale, exhaustion would finally overtake our eyelids. The next morning, Mom would rise early and start breakfast using whatever ingredients were left in the fridge. "Get up, you guys!" she'd yell, as the smell of coffee wafted through our town house. As we lumbered toward the bathroom to brush our teeth, Mom scurried around the kitchen, usually frying eggs and filling her mug with far more French vanilla and caramel creamer than coffee. That's the way she has always liked her coffee. How sweet is *that*?

Even as I did everything I could to conquer my kip, I also continued my TOPs training — remember, that's the program that puts you on an elite path and allows the national staff at USA Gymnastics to track how well you're performing over the years. Every summer, TOPs gymnasts are tested on their flexibility and physical abilities. If you nail the state or regional tests by making it into the top percentile of gymnasts around the country, you get a major perk: you're invited for more testing at the National TOPs training camp in Houston, Texas — the ranch where you get to meet the legendary Márta Károlyi, national coordinator for the US women's gymnastics team. In addition to strength testing, you also get to perform your gymnastics skills on all four of the apparatuses. The judges score your routines, they add the results of your physical abilities test, and voilà — you just might have a shot at making what's called the TOPs A or TOPs

B team. Every December, the A team is invited back for an all-expense-paid training camp at the Houston ranch. You have to be at least nine to even work your way up to the national camp trip, and since I was just seven when I started TOPs, I was aiming for one of four levels created by USAG for girls under the age of nine—the diamond level, the gold level, the bronze level, and the "Thank you so much for your participation!" level.

In July 2003, Mom and I drove to Cliffwood, New Jersey, for my first TOPs state testing at Rebound Gymnastics. "I just know you're going to make the diamond level," Mom declared. About five of the other girls in my gym program were also there, all of us performing a rigorous series of exercises capable of wiping out even the fittest athlete. And if that isn't enough to make your stomach do an Arabian double-front layout, there's also a time clock running, which means you have to get through as many push-ups, pull-ups, leg lifts, and press handstands as you can in, say, sixty seconds. Mom looked on from the balcony as I completed my exercises. After the first six minutes, I could feel the sweat forming on my back.

Did I make the diamond level? Not exactly. I discovered my results when I received my first official gymnastics prize in the mail: a bronze-level certificate. Ah, man! I wanted that diamond level almost as much as I'd once wanted to find my diamond earring on that playground. But then again, I was pretty grateful just to be recognized—at least I made the bronze level.

Once I was home from Jersey, it was time to get back to my kip. On Friday nights, there was open gym, a time when we could come to refine our skills or even just play outside of structured training. So Mom brought me to the gym one Friday so that I could keep working on my kip. "Need some help?" one of the higher-level girls asked when she saw me struggling. I nodded. So she and a few of the other gymnasts came over to coach me. By the end of that open gym session, I had mastered the skill! I hate to get all sentimental on you, but I actually got a warm feeling inside when I did my first kip. And here's a tip for all you aspiring gymnasts: A great kip is all about perfect timing, momentum, and strength.

My feeling of achievement was only temporarily replaced by a tingling sensation; a huge blister had formed on my palm. Later, when I showed Mom my hand with the blister now ripped wide open, she wailed, "Oooh, that's gross!" But I was proud of it. Why? Because Coach Dana had once told us this: "Getting a rip is a sign that you're a real gymnast."

So many times in life, we're faced with a choice: When a task becomes super difficult, will we flip out and quit, or will we stay focused and keep fighting? And then there's the question I often ask myself: How much will I trust in my Savior to lift me from the low bar to the higher one? The answer often depends on the day, my mood, the season. But every now and then, I actually do rely on God's strength instead of mine—and that's exactly the moment when I become a kipper.

Chapter Five

Progress is impossible without change.
—GEORGE BERNARD SHAW, PLAYWRIGHT

"MY DAUGHTER IS BECOMING STAGNANT." MOM PEERED STRAIGHT INTO the eyes of the owner of Gymstrada. He didn't blink. "Gabrielle is frustrated because she's not learning enough skills," Mom continued. "She needs more."

It was now 2004. After months of training to compete at Level 4, I was winning. A lot. And as much time as my two coaches, Dana and Amanda, spent on helping me refine my skills, I still couldn't believe how quickly that work was paying off: I grabbed gold at every single one of my six or seven meets that season. That's when I got my first big sniff of what it meant to train hard, compete even harder, and score victory. So as time marched on, I wasn't willing to settle for being good enough, or even going home with a medal. I wanted to master the difficult skills that would make me the best. In short, I wanted to rock my sport.

"I don't want to give her too much too fast," the owner finally said to Mom. "That will burn her out early." Mom accepted that explanation at first—but I didn't want to hear it. While I was training with the group of other eight-year-olds, out of the corner of my eye, I could see what was happening across the gym. The older girls were already learning a whole set of difficult skills, like a double layout on the floor and round-off back handspring back double back. I knew I was ready to push myself to master those same skills. How did I know it? I just had a strong feeling in my heart—kinda like an intuition.

The more competitions I won, the more I heard a particular sentence pop up over and over: "You're the next Dominique Dawes." I was like, "Who's *that*?" One evening, Mom said, "Google it." I did—and what I saw sent my lower jaw straight to my bedroom floor. Dominique was the powerhouse gymnast who rocked women's artistic gymnastics at the Olympics in 1992 (Barcelona), 1996 (Atlanta), and 2000 (Sydney). At the 1996 games, when the Magnificent Seven seized gold, Dominique was the only gymnast who had all eight of her scores count toward the team's total. When I pulled up Dominique's competition videos on YouTube, I witnessed firsthand just how much of a gifted and intense competitor she was: Her tumbling passes on the floor exercise often included ten (amazing!) skills in a row—from one corner of the spring mat to the next, and then all the way back again. And did I mention that she also tumbled her way into the history books? Dominique is the first black woman of *any* nationality to win an Olympic gold medal in women's artistic gymnastics. Amazing!

I was so inspired by Dominique's performance that it made me even more resolute in my campaign. I had to get my coaches to teach me bigger skills. "Please, Mom!" I pleaded. Little by little, Mom began to see my big point: If I was already winning so many competitions, why shouldn't my coaches be willing to take me to the next level as soon as I was ready to go there? At last, Mom scheduled another conversation—this time with Alex, a coach who'd once overseen the Romanian national team.

Meanwhile, another gigantic test rolled around: I had to get ready for a state competition, which takes place every spring at the end of the competitive season. In gymnastics, you can't just roll up at a state championship if you are a Level 4 gymnast; you have to first earn a qualifying score at what's called a sectional meet. I earned that score, and that meant I had the chance to battle it out for gold alongside the other gymnasts in my age group.

"Is this too much?" Coach Dana asked as she held a can of glitter hairspray above my ponytail and helped me get dressed. "A little more!" I answered. In the full-length mirror, I admired my long-sleeved leo, which was blue, black, and dotted with rhinestones—not bad! And I just loved the way the metallic-blue glitter stood out against my dark hair, which was pulled up in its usual scrunchie. You could call this one of my first baby steps from tomboy to girlie girl—realizing that glitter is pretty cool. "Are you nervous?" Dana asked. I was. At eight, I didn't fully understand what it meant to be a state champion, but I knew a big prize was on the line, and I wanted to win. And, of course, I still had the same questions that every other person alive has when they're facing something big: Will I do a good enough job? Will my hard work show? And what if I slip, mess up, or fall flat on my butt?

On one May afternoon, I got my answer — and I didn't once hit the floor, except to nail my landings! I accomplished what might've looked impossible for a four-pound, coughing, vomiting, wheezing child who'd once been diagnosed with a potentially fatal disease: I won the Level 4 all-around gymnastics competition and became the Virginia State Champion.

Arielle spotted a big box in front of her bedroom door one afternoon when she arrived home from school. *Scratch, scratch* came a noise from inside the box. Arielle slowly lifted the sides of the container and peeked inside. What could it be? As it turns out, it was something she'd been begging Mom to get us for weeks: a baby rabbit. "Thank you, Mom!" Arielle squealed when our mother walked through our front door that evening. "He's sooo cute!" He had the darkest coat of spotless fur I'd ever seen. That's why Arielle named him Midnight.

Midnight hopped into our lives at exactly the right moment — mostly because he provided a break from stress in the form of comic relief. "Get down from there,

Midnight!" — that was the sentence heard constantly around our home. Every time we'd let him out of his cage, he'd look around, pop his ears straight up into the air, and … *leeaaaaaaap*! In fact, Midnight leapt his way through every corner of our three-bedroom town house. We'd often find him hiding out under the bunk beds in my room or sniffing around for scraps of food that might make for a snack. "Come here, Midnight!" I'd hold on to our pet rabbit and run my tiny finger through his thick fur. But almost every time I pulled him close, he wiggled right out of my arms — and straight back down to the floor so he could begin his next adventure. Even when he wasn't quite in my view because he was hiding behind the shower curtain, Midnight was one of the bright spots of my time away from the gym — or maybe I should say dark spot.

Some Sundays, in place of going to church, Mom gathered us all around for Bible study. We took turns reading passages from Mom's old, brown-leather copy of the Amplified Bible. I had my favorites, starting with a brave man named Daniel. Back in Babylonian times, Daniel, a praying man, was given a top gig because he was such a hard worker. Some of his co-workers didn't like this very much, so they got together and plotted out how they could take him down. Their plan? Getting King Darius to pass a law that would send anyone caught praying to God straight to the lion's den. None of this stopped Daniel from praying — and soon after, he was indeed thrown into a ferocious den of hungry, spitting, growling lions. Early the next morning, the king, who'd realized he'd been tricked into signing that law by Daniel's colleagues, swung by to check on Daniel. And here's how the story picks up in Daniel 6:20–23 (NKJV):

"Daniel, servant of the living God, has your God, whom you serve continually, been able to deliver you from the lions?"

Then Daniel said to the king, "O king, live forever! My God sent His angel and shut the lions' mouths, so that they have not hurt me, because I was found innocent before Him; and also, O king, I have done no wrong before you."

Now can you see why I love Daniel? He wasn't afraid to stand his ground, even when he was dragged to the front door of a dingy den—or when he faced a whole slew of powerful lions. And that's because he knew that he had a power greater than any other in the world—the power of God's protection. "God didn't leave or fail Daniel, and He will never leave or fail you," Mom told us after she'd shut the Bible. "And because He's in your heart too, He will never fail you."

Another Big D has always topped my list of biblical faves: David, the sheep herder turned Israeli warrior. The Philistines and Israelites camped out for battle on two sides of a valley. And every day, the Philistines talked some serious trash: They sent over Goliath, a nine-foot-plus giant, to challenge the Israelites to step up and fight. Goliath did this twice a day for forty days straight. One day, David, then just a teen, was sent by his father to the front battle lines to find out how his brothers were surviving. When David got there, he heard Goliath dishing out his usual round of jeers. That's when skinny David did the unthinkable: He volunteered to fight the beefy Goliath. King Saul, who was understandably reluctant at first, finally agreed to let David try. Without even a stitch of armor, David gathered up five stones from a brook and placed them into his shepherd's pouch. "Then David said to the Philistine, 'You come to me with a sword, with a spear, and with a javelin. But I come to you in the name of the LORD of hosts, the God of the armies of Israel, whom you have defied"(1 Samuel 17:45, NKJV). That's when David took one last look at the burly hulk, removed a pebble from his pouch, placed it in a slingshot, pointed it straight at Goliath's forehead, and—pop!—took him down. Talk about guts.

After David slayed that giant, he didn't exactly live a squeaky-clean life—he did some downright rotten things, like steal another man's wife. That's why it's worth pointing out that God still called David a man after His own heart (Acts 13:22). "You mean we don't have to be perfect to please God?" I once asked Mom. "None of us is perfect," Mom answered. "That's why we need grace. No matter what we've done, He can always use us." Got it.

Mom sat across from Alex, the Romanian coach who'd joined Gymstrada's staff earlier that season. "My daughter is ready for the next level," Mom told him as Round Two of her crusade. "She needs more difficult skills." Alex knew Mom was right, but he also knew he shouldn't contradict what the gym's owner had already told Mom. "Look, I can't really tell you what to do," Alex finally said. "But I will tell you this: You've got to do your own homework. You've got to take your daughter's career into your own hands from this point on."

As comfortable as it is to hold on to what's familiar, we sometimes have to move on in order to move up. I knew it. Mom knew it. Alex knew it. And in June 2004, after I'd become Virginia State Champion, I finally ended my time at Gymstrada and began training down the street at Excalibur Gymnastics. What came next began a bold new chapter for me—one filled with some of the biggest challenges of my gymnastics training.

Around the same time, a few weeks after we got our pet rabbit, Midnight, Mom mistakenly fed him some strawberry-flavored oatmeal—don't be made at her, 'cause it was truly an accident! Arielle came home to find Midnight's furry body lying paws-up in his cage. The following Sunday, we all moped around the house in our PJs, saddened by the loss of our beloved bunny—and no one was more upset than our mother. A few weeks later, our grief was replaced by a second surprise: Mom brought home another rabbit, Midnight's brother. Okay, so he wasn't nearly as charming as Midnight—that's how he ended up with the name Shadow!—but he stilled filled the empty space in Midnight's cage. And on our living room sofa. And in our hearts.

Beginnings and endings, endings and beginnings — that's just the way life goes. And whether or not we like what happens after we've taken a courageous step forward, we can always count on one thing: The next experience will forever change us. Just ask David.

Chapter Six

It is a terrible thing to see and have no vision.
—HELEN KELLER, DEAF-BLIND ACTIVIST

JUST ABOUT EVERY OLYMPIC ATHLETE CAN TELL YOU EXACTLY WHEN HE or she caught the fervor—that intense desire to compete in the Olympics. Michael Phelps felt the fire when he watched Tom Dolan swim for gold in the 1996 Atlanta games. Jamaican sprinter Usain Bolt got his shot of lightning at age twelve, when his high school PE teacher, Lorna Thorpe, noticed his raw talent and pushed him to pursue track and field. My big dose of inspiration came on August 19, 2004—the Thursday evening when gymnast Carly Patterson showed up on my family's television screen.

"Look, Mom," I shrieked, scurrying from the sofa and onto my tiptoes. "Carly's doing giants!" The giant is a skill that involves swinging around and around the uneven bars—and it was the very skill I was learning on the bars that season. As my entire family sat huddled around our TV, I kept tapping my mother. "Guess what,

Mom—I'm doing that!" After I'd cut in about seven more times, my mother went, "Okay, Gabrielle. Just watch the Olympics!"

In the days leading up to that evening, sports commentators everywhere had repeated a single question: Will Carly Patterson become the next Mary Lou Retton? As thousands gathered in the Olympic Sports Complex Indoor Hall in Athens, Greece—and millions more around the world tuned in—that question would be answered at the women's all-around finals.

The stakes were beyond high. Carly, who came to the Olympics with a World Champion team title, faced off against three-time World all-around champion Svetlana Khorkina of Russia. On vault, Carly attempted a double-twisting Yurchenko that earned her a score of 9.375—a bit of a shaky start. During the next two rotations, Svetlana took the lead. But Carly rebounded with strong performances on the uneven bars (9.575) and the balance beam (9.725—thanks to an Arabian double front dismount that she punctuated with a perfect landing). The moment that Carly placed her ankles just inside the boundaries of the spring mat as the last gymnast to compete in floor exercise, she knew the minimum score she needed in order to go home with a gold—a 9.536.

Carly saluted the judges. She then shook her hips to the initial notes of Big Bad Voodoo Daddy's upbeat song "Mr. Pinstripe Suit" and leapt into her first tumbling pass. I could visualize Americans everywhere sucking in a collective breath as she powerfully hurled her body through the air … and … "She nailed it!" Mom yelled. It all came down to the last of Carly's four tumbling passes. After she thrust her five-foot frame into the air, flipped across the mat with her ponytail swinging, and landed on her feet, Carly's huge smile afterward said it all—she knew she'd grabbed the gold.

Seconds later, Carly's official score appeared on the board above—9.712, a number indeed high enough to nudge Svetlana into silver territory. That night, as Carly had that gold medal placed around her neck, she didn't become the next Mary Lou—she became the first Carly Patterson. She also became the gymnast who widened my vision for what I could accomplish in my sport, just as Dominique Dawes had done. I suddenly had my sights set on a single goal: I wanted to stand on top of that podium. That night, I made a choice—I would work harder than ever at the new gym I'd joined just two months before.

We were late—and I absolutely hate to be late. It makes me so crabby. I could feel my heart rate quicken as Mom weaved through traffic at eight in the morning to get us to Excalibur Gymnastics for my first day of training. *What impression would we make by being late on the first day?* I thought. My friend Kaiya, who was making the switch to the new gym with me, sat next to me in the backseat. When we finally pulled into the parking lot at 8:03, I sighed and glanced over at Kaiya. I guess three minutes late wasn't so bad.

Excalibur seemed so much larger than my old gym. On one side of the gym stood an oversized mirror, and its reflection made the room seem far more spacious than it probably was. Sunlight poured through three enormous windows and made the room glow. It was so bright in there! I looked up to notice dozens of flags from all over the world—places like Argentina, Chile, China, and Japan. And of course, I spotted lots of apparatuses spread around the gym: beams, trampolines, uneven bars standing over a foamy, squishy pit, and a brand-new bouncy floor. A group of about twenty girls—all at different skill levels and ages—lined up so that Kaiya and I could greet them. Each girl said her name as we worked our way down the line—but by the end, I couldn't remember a single one.

"Walking handstands, everyone!" Jim Walker, one of the coaches at Excalibur, called out after we'd divided up in our levels. Kaiya lowered her palms to the floor. A moment later, I did the same. Over the next ten seconds, we walked as far as we could on our hands, trying so hard not to fall—because falling meant we had to start over. Once we completed that exercise (no falls, thank you!), we moved on to the uneven bars. I mounted the bars, attempted a move called a free hip—then came crashing to the floor. "Are you okay?" asked Jim, who rushed to my side. "Yeah, I'm good," I said with a giggle—the same giggle I used to let out as a toddler when I'd crash on our living room. "Oh, man—you're a tough one!" Jim said.

During my first days at Excalibur in June 2004, I was

already on a mission: I wanted to learn as many new skills as I could before the TOPs testing in July. Yes, I'd been winning championships, but because TOPs requires such a high level of difficulty, the skills I'd already mastered simply weren't impressive enough to help me make the TOPs A team. A perfect example of that? Gustavo, who was one of my coaches—along with his wife, Marina—asked my group to do ten press handstands on the beam. I could only do about three correctly. "Keep trying," the coach said. My heart sank as I watched all the other gymnasts move on to the other rotations—and I had to stay on the beam because I was struggling so much with my skill. I knew I had to get better.

Let me tell you how determined I was: I must've practiced that handstand one hundred times over the next two days. And by the third day, I did what even my coach found unfathomable: I knocked out ten perfect press handstands. Was I going to be left behind? Not a chance. My mother's a fighter. My siblings are fighters. And during that first week at Excalibur, I proved to myself that I was also a fighter. I not only mastered my handstand, I also fought my way onto the TOPs A team. That meant that I would be at training camp alongside girls who'd already been competing at Levels 7 and 8 for months. Yikes.

I used to be Jewish. Well, not *exactly* Jewish—but my family practiced some of the Jewish traditions. For a reason that she still can't explain, my mother has always felt drawn to Judaism—even when she was a child. Her mother felt the same unexplainable pulls; she sometimes prepared kosher meals. When she was just fourteen, Mom asked my grandmom, "Can we go to the synagogue?" They didn't, but they still incorporated a bit of Jewish culture alongside their Christian faith.

Back when we lived in Texas, Mom began studying under Billye Brim, a minister who'd traveled to Israel in 1986, learned Hebrew, and studied with rabbis. Billye Brim eventually returned to America to teach some of the principles of Judaism from a Christian perspective. Mom attended a couple of her conferences. "I saw some parallels between Judaism and Christianity," Mom says now. "Studying Judaism gave me a greater understanding of what I'd been taught over the years, and it actually strengthened my faith in God."

In 2004, Mom took her interest in Judaism to a new level: she studied Hebrew and began taking me, Arielle, Joyelle, and John to Temple Israel, a synagogue in Norfolk. Every weekend, we celebrated Shabbat, the holy Jewish day of rest that begins on Friday evening and ends on Saturday evening. Sometimes, we visited other local synagogues in the area—and during one service, we formed a circle, held hands, and danced exuberantly to a song the leaders taught us. So fun!

Our weekly trips to the synagogue eventually faded, partly because Mom's Nissan Altima broke down, meaning we couldn't drive there to attend services. Then Mom had to work extra hours on the weekends to save up for another car. Even still, Mom encouraged us to continue studying our faith. "I'm not going to choose a path for you," Mom told us, "but I want you to always explore the truth. God gives us all free will to choose what we will believe."

Long after our last Shabbat celebration, my love for Jewish culture continued—so rich and beautiful. One tradition that'll probably always stick around in our family is Mom's homemade matzo ball soup—she makes a mean version of it! At first, Mom would only make the soup during Passover, a holiday when Jews remember how the ancient Israelites were freed from slavery. But we all loved her soup so much that we begged her to cook it for every special occasion—like if Arielle or John made the honor roll, if Joy performed well in an ice skating competition, or if I got the highest score at a meet. Sometimes, Mom wouldn't tell us she was stirring up her recipe—but I'd come running into the kitchen because I could smell it. "You're making the soup, aren't you?" I'd ask with a grin. Then we'd gather around our table, elbow to elbow, and savor each huge spoonful.

The year I was nine, we celebrated Hanukkah. Mom even bought us each a dreidel, a four-sided spinning top. As we played with our new toys, the music from our new CD (remember those?) filled the town house. "Twinkle, twinkle, candle bright," the melody went, "burning on the special night." My siblings and I were cool with celebrating Hanukkah—until we realized that we wouldn't celebrate Christmas or decorate a tree. "Does this also mean we won't get presents?" I asked Mom. "No," she said. "It means you get a present for eight days straight." And yet both then and now, some of my best gifts haven't come wrapped in a box. They're things like laughing until I'm literally weak after Joyelle tells me a hilarious story. Or climbing into Mom's bed and hanging out with my whole family. Or getting major goose bumps when I saw Carly win the gold.

The Second Marriage

One day in late March 2005, Mom gathered all four of us in the living room. "Tim and I are getting remarried," she said matter-of-factly. She then looked directly at John, Joyelle, and me. "That's right—your dad and I are going to try and work things out." My first feeling was one of excitement. *At last, my parents will be together,* I thought. *I'll get to see my father every day*—because at this point, I hadn't seen him for at least a year. It quickly became clear that my older sister Arielle had an altogether different opinion. "This is a big mistake," she told Mom. The rest of us fell completely silent. "Why is it going to work out so much better this time, Mom?" Our mother paused before she finally responded. "Arielle, Tim is the father of these three children," she said slowly. "I really want to make this work."

That conversation was my first glimpse into a world that only Arielle understood: She'd been old enough to recall what it felt like to be cold and homeless in that Dodge van in Tulsa. During that time, my father had worked sporadically—and Arielle wanted to be sure that if Mom married him again, he would have a steady paycheck to contribute to the household.

"Does he have a job?" Arielle pressed.

"We'll be fine," Mom said. "I have some money saved up." In late April, I came home after a double session at the gym to find my father sitting in the living room of our town house. All at once, I felt elated and stunned.

Chapter Seven

A problem is a chance for you to do your best.
—DUKE ELLINGTON, JAZZ LEGEND

I REALLY WANTED TO IMPRESS MÁRTA KÁROLYI — AND CAN YOU BLAME me? She and her husband, Bela, are huge legends in the sport of gymnastics. Bela once coached Romanian sensation Nadia Comãneci, the gymnast who scored seven (yes, seven!) perfect 10.0s at the 1976 Olympics in Montreal, Quebec. In 1981, Bela and Márta left their homeland of Romania and sought political asylum in America. Between the two of them, they've trained nine Olympic champions, including Mary Lou Retton, the first American woman to ever win the all-around gold. So when any young gymnast meets Márta — who has been the powerhouse national team coordinator for USA gymnastics since 2001 — it's not quite like chillaxing at the beach. It's more like nail-biting at the ranch.

Make that the Károlyi ranch — a US Olympic training center that Bela built on about two thousand acres north of

Houston. Tucked away in the forest stands a fifty-thousand-square-foot gymnasium, the place where the best gymnasts in the world have been trained. I had my first turn at the ranch in December 2004, the year I made the national TOPs A team.

My road to Texas was more like a superhighway. I've already told you that when I arrived at Excalibur in June 2004, I had a ton of catching up to do when it came to skills. Well here's the part I left out: I had just a few weeks to prepare for TOPs A testing that July. And even as I pushed myself to my physical limits during that summer, my 2004–2005 season was also revving up in the fall. So between summer and the end of the year, I made the biggest gymnastics leap I've ever made during any one period of time—I jumped from a Level 4 to a Level 7, the first of the levels in which I could design my own routine. Let me break that down for you in English (well, sorta): In just a few months, I went from doing basic split jumps, handsprings, and glide swings to performing at least two circling skills on bars, a front walkover on beam, and a back layout on floor. In a word, difficult.

The great news is that I earned a spot on the TOPs A national team. The slightly unnerving news (at least for me, a perfectionist) is that I barely made the cut. "I could've done better," I told my mother. "I messed up on some of the skills." Mom responded the way she has so many times. "Yes, you're almost dead last going into the camp, which is why you've gotta be willing to work your way to the top," she said. "No one's ever going to give you anything. There are no excuses. There's just hard work."

After I made the TOPs A national team, I was invited back to the ranch for the training camp in December. That's when I did my best to show Márta just how well I could perform. "Good job, Little One!" Márta said when she saw me showing off every single skill I knew. "Little One" was Márta's first nickname for me—the second would come later!—because she noticed how much smaller I was compared to the other gymnasts. She'd sometimes hold my entire face between her two hands or pat me on the head when she called me by that nickname. Any little bit of affirmation from Márta—and I do mean any—meant so much to me. Especially since I could look around camp and spot girls who were rising Level 8s. At first, that scared me a little. *Will I be good enough to compete?* But with some encouragement from Mom, I realized something: the only way to keep growing is to continually put yourself in situations where you'll be stretched. And that kind of stretching isn't usually all that comfortable.

Once I was back from training camp, Mom signed me up for a ballet class—talk about a stretch. As I honed my gymnastics skills, Mom wanted me to add a touch of ballerina grace to my floor routines. "These are itchy," I complained when I slid on each leg of my pink ballerina tights before class. I was like, "Mom, when is this over?" That whole experiment only lasted a couple months— and if you ask me, that was two months too long!

I've always been an animal lover. When I was small, I was always trying to bring home stray dogs in our neighborhood. "No, Brie," my sisters told me when I once tried to rescue a puppy. "What if he has rabies?" I still tried to take him home, but Mom wouldn't let me keep him.

One evening after a double session when Kaiya's mom, Kim, couldn't pick us up from the gym, her dad met us instead. "We're going to the pet store to visit the animals," he announced, and I could feel my heart skip a beat. Once there, Kaiya fell head over heels for a dog we spotted. Later, her dad got her a dog mixed with everything from poodle to Schnauzer, which she named Mugsy. "He *sooo* cute!" I told Kaiya. Whenever I visited Mugsy at Kaiya's house, I felt a pang of jealousy shoot through me. That's when the same thought I'd been having for months hit me again: *Why can't we get a puppy?*

When I brought it up to Mom on our way home, her answer was the same—definitely not. The closest I came to having my very own set of four furry little paws that year was the following Christmas: Mom got me a stuffed black dog.

For months, I kept lobbying. "You should see how adorable Mugsy is!" I told her. Mom still said no, yet the fact that she usually said it with a hint of a smile told me there was a crack in the door. "Please, Mom!" I said. "Kaiya's parents even got her a pet puppy." But no matter how thick I laid on the guilt, it wasn't enough to convince our mother.

Until one August day in 2005. That afternoon, Mom showed up at my gym holding a box. When I saw a piece of black fur peeking out from under the sides, I put my hand over my heart. *Could it be?* "Surprise!" Mom said when she lifted the lid. It was another stuffed dog.

"Oh, thanks," I said, trying to squelch a tone of disappointment.

"Don't you like him?" Mom asked.

"Um, yes," I said as I forced a smile. A few minutes later, we walked out to our car. John and Joyelle, who'd come along with Mom to pick me up, were waiting in the backseat. "Hi, guys," I said as I climbed into the front. Just then, I spotted the most amazing sight my ten-year-old eyes had ever seen: a real puppy bounced up from behind Joyelle and John.

"I can't believe it!" I squealed. I literally began jumping up and down, finally landing long enough to wrap both my arms all the way around his warm body. The pup was an eight-week-old black Labrador and Rottweiler mix that Mom got from a local Society for the Prevention of Cruelty to Animals (SPCA). Go, Mom!

We all drove to Arielle's school and tried to pull the same trick on her. When she came outside after cheer-leading practice, she didn't go for the gag—but even still, she was just as excited as we all were about our dog, who we named Zoway. I don't think Zoway's paws touched the ground the entire first day we got him, and I could relate: I was on cloud nine hundred with no chance of coming back down to earth anytime soon.

A few years later, after Kaiya got a second dog (a Chihuahua), Joy and I began plotting how we could grow our family by one as well. We found an Internet photo of the cutest Toy Yorkie and printed it out. Along the bottom of that paper, I used a Magic Marker to write out the name we'd already picked for our dog: Chandler. We then hung that photo smack-dab in the center of the refrigerator door so Mom would see it every time she went into the kitchen. "You are not getting another dog," our mother announced when she saw the photo for the first time. I tried every angle I could think of: "If I get all As, can we *pleeeease* get him?" Or this one, my favorite: "Can I have another puppy if I win my next meet?" But none of it worked.

Then one afternoon when Mom picked me up after the first half of a double session, I was actually done with my homework—so Mom and I had a little time to burn.

"Where should we go?" she asked me.

"Let's go to the pet store in Pembroke Mall," I said. "That's where Kaiya's dad takes us when we have extra time before going back to the gym." Mom hesitated but turned out of the lot and onto the road leading to the mall. Once we got inside the Pet-Go-Round store, I headed straight to the back. There, a group of puppies, all with light brown and white fur, pranced about in a glass cage. A sign taped to the outside of the case read *Morkies*—a mix between a Maltese and a Yorkie.

"Would you like to hold one?" a saleslady asked me.

"Yes!" I said emphatically. That's when she scooped up the tiniest puppy in the bunch and put him right into my arms.

"I'll take you to the back here so that you two can get

better acquainted," the saleswoman said as she led us to a playroom.

"Can we take him home, Mom?" I could tell by the look on my mother's face that she'd known that question was coming.

"No, Brie," she said. "Unfortunately, the puppy needs to go back into his temporary home. But he's so cute that I know it won't take long before he finds a loving home." Mom then handed the puppy back to the salesperson. Then, just as we were leaving the store, I looked back to see the dog leaping up to the top of the cage as if he was begging me to come back for him.

"Look, Mom!" I said. "He wants to go home with us!"

Mom paused—and the moment she turned around to see the same thing I saw, I knew it was a done deal. After Mom had a couple days to come around, I finally got Chandler—make that Channie or Chan Chan, which is what I called him for short.

So that's how Zoway got a little brother—and how we remember that our mother is as soft as she is strong.

The more I trained for competition at high levels, the more time I spent at the gym—and the less time I got to hang out with my family. Mom began working back-to-back shifts, and I'd see her briefly when she picked me up at five each afternoon. At home, Arielle, then a sophomore at Landstown High, played latchkey mom. She was the first to arrive at our town house, then she made sure

Joyelle and John made it home, did their homework, and ate some dinner. At ten o'clock, Mom finally dragged herself home from her second shift.

My many hours at the gym also meant lots of moolah—which is why Mom was working so much. Some say that gymnastics is a sport for the affluent: the wristbands, the grips, the tape, and the tuition for the training time can all add up to thousands every year. That's because things like grips, which run about $50 a pop, have to be replaced regularly, or else they'll rip and put you in danger on the bars. Competition leos are usually $200 and up, and practice leos (we call them tanks) are about $50. Then there are meet fees and travel expenses, as well as the cost of hiring someone to choreograph a floor routine. Speaking of which, Mom once paid $600 for my choreography—and when a coach didn't like it very much, Mom had to shell out another $600 for me to get a new one.

Back during my Gymstrada days, Mom was part of the Gymnastics Parent Association (completely separate from the gym) that created fund-raisers to offset the high cost of training. The group's major source of income: hosting Saturday night bingo games for the public. The parents took their turns in a rotation, and Mom did her part once or twice a month. At the bingo hall, Mom often worked at the back of the room as a money counter. "I have bad allergies," Mom says now, "so I couldn't stand all that smoke up at the front!"

Since that time when we were homeless in Tulsa, Mom was definitely doing a little better financially, thanks to the double shifts. But because she was the only bread-winner for our family, her checking account funds were often low. She'd saved up every quarter she had to get us into our small town house, but it was right on the edge of a rough area. We were surrounded by parties with lots of drinking and smoking; the thumpity-thump of loud music often kept us awake at night. Sometimes, we even heard gunshots and witnessed drug deals and gang activity. Though the Virginia Beach Police Department cracked down on the crime and really cleaned up our area over the years, back then, Scarborough Square was still seen by many as a very tough neighborhood. So whenever I visited the homes of some of my Excalibur teammates for the end-of-the-season parties, I realized just how different our circumstances were. For starters, their homes were massive—and usually in the best parts of town.

You want to hear something shocking? I was still thankful for what we had—and yes, I actually mean that. Would it have been nice to get more of the extras at times? Of course. Yet what I did have was my brother, John, to jump with me on the trampoline for hours in our backyard. What I did have was my sister, Arielle, who let me hide my stash of Tootsie Rolls in her bedroom so that Joyelle and John wouldn't steal them. And what I did have was a mother who taught me to hold on tightly to 2 Timothy 1:7 whenever I was feeling a tad jittery: "For God has not given us the spirit of fear, but of power and of love and of a sound mind" (NKJV).

The Gifts

Mother's Day was coming—and we all wanted to get our mother a special gift.

"What should we buy?" I asked my father.

"Let's look around and see what we can find."

So while Mom was at home catching some much needed zzz's, Dad loaded all of us into the car and headed to Walmart. Once inside, we filled our cart with so many different presents: a silk robe, slippers, a foot massager, flowers, a set of dishes, and even a crystal candleholder. As Dad loaded the bags into the car, I told Joy, "Mom is going to be so surprised!"

So you can imagine my shock when Mom later blew up. "Take it back!" she screamed at my father. "Take it all back, Tim!"

John, Joy, and I shuffled off to our bedroom and closed the door for a private discussion. "Why is Mom being so mean to Dad?" I asked. "All he wanted to do was give her some presents!" That's when Arielle came in, saw us huddling, and interrupted. "You guys don't understand," she said. "Your dad spent money we don't have. Of course Mom likes the presents. She just doesn't want our water to be shut off."

"You're adopted!" shouted Joyelle, who was angry at my sister's assessment and feeling defensive of our dad. "You're not even the same skin color as the rest of us!"

That was enough to make Arielle storm out of the room. I stayed put, only to keep thinking over the one big question I had back then: Why did my mother dislike my dad so much? I was as confused as I was sad. Dad rebagged all the gifts and took them back to Walmart that same afternoon.

Chapter Eight

No weapon formed against you shall prosper.
—Isaiah 54:17, NKJV

I TRIED SO HARD TO BE NICE TO THE OTHER GIRLS AT EXCALIBUR. YET as my skill level improved and I surpassed some of my teammates, I noticed something: a few of them seemed a lot less friendly. I'm not talking about the majority of them, of course—there were plenty of cool girls at the gym. So how could I tell which ones didn't like me? Sometimes I'd see them whispering, but they'd suddenly stop talking if I came near. Other times, they wouldn't look directly at me. I'm sure you can just feel it when someone doesn't like you—and believe me, I felt it.

For a long time, I kept everything inside. My family was already giving up so much for me to be a gymnast, and I didn't want to burden Mom with one more thing. I also didn't want to start a big drama with the other girls by bringing it up to my coaches. I knew that would make the other gymnasts dislike me even more. In competitive gymnastics, you're taught to be strong and handle whatever might stand in the way of your training. So because I loved my sport so much—and because I didn't want to seem like a tattletale—I just dealt with my feelings of isolation.

Yet ignoring the situation didn't make it disappear. There were certain tasks my teammates and I took turns doing before we started training, and one day it was one of the other gymnast's turn to scrape all the excess chalk off the uneven bars. That's when the girl said, "Why doesn't Gabby do it? She's our slave." I looked over to see the girl standing there with this smirk on her face. I could feel my stomach muscles tighten and my heart sink. I wanted to cry—but I didn't. Instead, I just stared at her.

"That's not cool," another gymnast said to the girl.

"Well, you make jokes all the time too," the girl shot back.

"I do," the other gymnast said, "but not that kind of joke. You should never joke about something like that."

When I got home that evening, all my pent-up emotion came pouring out. I shut the door to my bedroom and prayed. "God, what did I do to deserve that comment?" I said between sobs. "And why are they being so mean to me?" Later, when Mom arrived home from work, she asked how my day went. "Fine," I fibbed. Not until much later did I find the courage to tell her the whole story.

Especially during this time, my strong friendship with Kaiya became a lifeline.

"Did you finish your math homework yet?" she asked

me one afternoon. I hated math—and she knew it—so we both let out a you-know-better-than-that giggle. Kaiya and I were both homeschooled—after I finished second grade at Holland Elementary, I did homeschool from third grade on. For a competitive gymnast, homeschool is often more like *gym* school—in between my training time, I followed an online curriculum. During my first year in homeschool, I used a book curriculum called A Beka, the same one used at Greenhill Farms Academy. The second year, my mom moved me onto Alpha Omega, a CD/book interactive program.

As part of the homeschool life, parents provided their children with laptops—the first MacBook Mom got me was white! On-site tutors (and my mother, of course) guided me through the material and helped me with any homework I didn't understand. At Excalibur, I trained from eight to noon and then from two thirty to five o'clock, which meant I did my schoolwork between noon and two thirty—not a lot of time to mess around! At night when I came home from the gym, I did more homework. But sometimes I was too exhausted from all that training to touch a book.

Kaiya was a little older than me. So even though she could help me with my homework, I was zero help to her. (Sorry, Kaiya!) Maybe I couldn't solve her biology problems, but I could provide a little comic relief—and we laughed constantly. Sometimes, we pretended we were in real school and passed silly notes back and forth to each other. The teacher who was handling that subject for our group would overhear us whispering and say, "Get to work, you two!"—and that usually made us laugh even harder.

In addition to history, I enjoyed science. Why? Because I got to do experiments and mix chemicals and make bubbles—and I could use the concoctions to pull pranks on my sisters and brother . . . ha, ha, just kidding! I also loved speech class. When I was small, I couldn't say the word *rabbit*—I pronounced it as *wabbit*. By the end of that class, my teacher had corrected my pronunciation—plus, she gave me a lot of cool stuff, like a coupon for a free pizza in the café. My all-time favorite teacher was Mr. Dule, a bald-headed African American man. He was so intense. In his PE class, I ripped my way up the hanging rope with such a fast speed; I then cranked out pull-ups like there was no tomorrow. He was in awe of my strength. He set up a lot of fun obstacle courses for our class, and sometimes, he even joined in to finish the course with us. Because I had gymnastics training, the whole class was easy as pie!

We hardly ever got snow in Virginia Beach. So on the few occasions when the glistening flakes fell from the heavens and blanketed our front yard, it felt like a holiday for my siblings and me. One winter, we'd all been dreaming of a white Christmas. Our dream came true a little late: on a January morning, we awakened to snowfall.

"Look, Joy!" I squealed when I spotted the flakes though a window early that morning. "It's *snowing*!"

My sister and I shared the bottom bunk, and John slept in the bunk above. Joy and I were so excited about the snow that we woke him up with our shrieks. Before Mom or Arielle could stumble out of bed, the three of us raced to put on our clothes and shoes. We then pulled on our heavy coats (the ones with the fur trim around the hood) and dashed out the back door.

Outside, we started a game we made up—a combination of tag and hide and go seek. "You're it!" I yelled at John. He then closed his eyes for a few moments, just long enough for Joyelle and me to find someplace to hide. It didn't take my brother very long to find me crouched behind the outdoor trampoline.

"You're it now, Brie!" he shouted.

Once we grew tired of our little game, we dropped to our knees and began gathering heaps of what looked like magic stardust. After a few minutes, we'd collected enough to build a medium-sized snowman.

Mom, who was finally up and having her usual coffee with way too much creamer, called us into the house.

"Put this outside and let it catch some fresh flakes," she said, handing us a large plastic bowl. An hour later, the bowl was overflowing with the cleanest, flakiest snow I've ever seen. After we'd thrown our last snowballs at each other (I loved sneakily putting chunks of snow down John's back!), we all dragged ourselves inside in our wet clothes. I handed Mom the bowl.

"I'm going to make something special for you," she said. She then mixed the bowl of flakes with a bit of sugar, added a touch of food coloring, and placed a perfectly rounded scoop of her creation into three small paper cups. (We all loved our treat so much that we begged Mom to make it every time it snowed. And as long as there was a homemade snow cone and a game of tag involved, a day in the snow was all we needed.)

After we'd traded our soaking shirts, jeans, and socks for dry sets, Joyelle and I then settled down in the living room and took out our dolls. One Christmas, Mom surprised me with Yasmin, a Bratz doll. On the Bratz TV series that Joy and I sometimes watched, Yasmin got the nickname Pretty Princess because she once kissed a toy frog.

"Isn't she just the cutest?" I said to my sis, who was busy pulling on her doll's blouse.

"She is!" Joyelle agreed.

I loved brushing Yasmin's hair and dressing her in all those adorable little miniskirts. I also loved her TV show character. On the series, Yasmin loved pets so much that she started an animal rescue program. A doll after my own heart!

Joyelle and I had quite a few TV show connections, actually. For instance, one of my favorite shows was *Wildfire*, about a girl named Kris who owns a horse. For years, I dreamed about mounting a horse and riding off on it, deep into the countryside. "I'm gonna get my own horse one day," I often told Joyelle.

"Well, *I'm* going to become a mermaid," she'd often reply. That's because we were both into a show called

H20: Just Add Water, which was the story of three teenage girls who happened to be Australian mermaids. Whenever we went to the pool, we'd even practice our mermaid swim.

But many of those games and conversations were during summer—which felt so, so far away during our big snow day that January. Outside our town house, the flakes began falling harder; Arielle was still in bed, snuggled tightly beneath her covers. Our mother brought us one last small homemade snow cone along with a cup of hot chocolate to warm up our hands.

"Mom, can we go back into the yard?" I begged. I thought we could upgrade our snowman with a few extra heaps of powder.

"I don't want you to catch a cold," said our mother, always the protective one. "Let's just enjoy the snow from inside." Mom and John then squeezed into a spot on our couch next to Joy and me, and we sat aside our dolls. For a few moments that I wish could've stretched into eternity, the four of us gazed silently out the window as a flurry of shimmering flakes cascaded toward the ground.

By now, you've probably caught on to something: my mother is always standing by with just the right Scripture or inspirational saying to get me through any tough situation. One of her favorites has always been two verses she used together: "The last will be first, and the first will be last. The LORD will make you the head, not the tail" (Matthew 20:16 and Deuteronomy 28:13, NIV).

When it came to TOPs, Mom's words turned out to be prophetic. The first time I tested for TOPs in 2004, I barely qualified at the bottom of the national stack—but hey, at least I made the cut. My second shot came in October 2005, and I landed smack-dab in the middle of my peers around the nation. The following year, I did something that still astounds Mom and my coaches: I not only qualified, but I also had the best score in the nation. Whoa!

I wanted to keep rising in my sport—but I had no idea that my ascent would be more like a dizzying catapult. I claimed gold in one competition after another ... after another ... after another. In 2005, I began training and competing at Level 8, and by the following spring, I was in first place at another Virginia State championship. Then in 2007, I rose to Level 9 and claimed the top spot on beam in the State Championships. The following spring, I started training at Level 10.

The summer I was eleven, I took a huge leap forward: I competed in the USA Challenge Hopes Pre-Elite program and placed first in the all-around. The Hopes Division was created for pre-elite gymnasts between the ages of ten and twelve—those who are on track to eventually move on to the junior elite and senior elite levels. And why is that important? Because once you make it to these highest levels, you're among that small group of gymnasts who are the very best in the world. That also means you're good enough to try out for the Olympic team.

Here's what I knew by the time I was twelve: something pretty amazing was happening in my life—and it was happening so much faster than me, my coaches, or even my mother could have predicted. Yes, I worked tirelessly at the gym, but so do a lot of gymnasts. So why had God chosen to give *me* this special gift? Maybe it's for the same reason that Mom asked us to gather snow—so she could create something really sweet to pass on.

The Closet

In 2006, my father left for his second eight-month deployment—this time, he was going to Iraq. A few months after he'd left for his overseas tour, I came home to find my mother packing. She was surrounded by enormous plastic bins, and she was pulling my father's shirts, pants, and shoes from the closet. Arielle was helping her.

"Mom, why are you packing Dad's stuff?" I asked.

She paused. "I'm just trying to make more room in the closet, Brie," she said. "Plus, I'm sending more clothes to your dad."

Not until years later did Mom tell me why she was really clearing out the closet: that was the very day she and my father had chosen to end their relationship forever. Their first marriage had lasted for nine years. Their second marriage had held together for just over a year, until constant arguments had weakened it beyond repair.

"I told Mom it wouldn't work," Arielle later said to me. At the time, all I knew was my father was never coming back to our town house to live with us. That afternoon, Mom and Arielle filled the plastic bins to overflowing and sealed them as tightly as they could.

Chapter Nine

In the middle of difficulty lies opportunity.
—ALBERT EINSTEIN

I LIKE MY NOSE. I ALWAYS HAVE. YET A FEW PAINFUL EXPERIENCES I HAD while at Excalibur really shook my confidence for a time—not just in the way my nose looked, but in the way I saw my gymnastics abilities.

During a typical training session at the gym one afternoon, my teammates and I were making our way through our skills and rotations. When I got about halfway through my exercises for the day, I overheard one of my coaches say something I'll never forget: "Yeah, she needs a nose job." He was talking to another coach, but he was definitely looking in my direction.

A string of thoughts sped through my head. *Why would my coach say such a cruel thing about me? Did he mean it? What was wrong with my nose? And why did he make that comment loud enough for me and my teammates to hear it?* I was so disturbed by what I heard that my heart felt like it was going to beat right out of my chest. I moved quickly through the remaining rotations and went home.

That night and for a long time afterward, I didn't tell my mother what happened—for all the same reasons I hadn't told her about the growing isolation I'd been feeling at the gym. As hurtful as my teammates' actions had been, this was worse. This time, the insult was coming from someone that I cared about and trusted—a coach who was supposed to have my best interest at heart.

The offensiveness didn't end there. A few weeks later, some of my teammates and I were at a party together—one of the social gatherings our coaches sometimes hosted at their homes. The coach who'd insulted me before was there. With me and a few other gymnasts gathered around, that coach turned to me and delivered the same shocking sentence: "You need a nose job." I stared at him in disbelief for what must've been a few seconds—but what felt like a thousand years. A moment later, a couple of my teammates broke the silence with a chuckle. But I didn't find anything funny. In fact, his comment stung me even more than it had the first time, because he said it directly to me.

A few days later, the same teammates who'd overheard my coach's comments brought it up again as a joke. "Your nose is so flat," one of them said, snickering. "How do you even breathe out of it?" I was so stunned by her words that I all could conjure up in response was a sarcastic, "Thanks, guys." I then simply turned and walked away.

Years later, when I finally opened up about these experiences, some people pointed out that I never reported the incidents back when they happened. That's true. But to fully comprehend why I didn't speak up, you have to understand the environment I was in. Any competitive gymnast can tell you that we're taught to be tough from a very young age—to suck it up and keep pressing toward our goal. Sure, if I would've revealed the mistreatment, the people involved may have been reprimanded. But if I then *stayed* at Excalibur, do you think my time there would've been easier—or harder? As a twelve-year-old, I reasoned that speaking up would make things more difficult and that would take my focus off perfecting my skills. That's why I kept the rude comments a secret.

Yet I couldn't completely cover up the impact that the words had on me. "Am I pretty, Mom?" I asked my mother one evening about a month after that party.

"Of course, Brie," she said. "You've always been beautiful."

But I was starting to have my doubts. "Was I cute even as a baby?" I pressed.

"Yes," she assured me. "Why are you asking me this?"

"Oh, it's nothing," I answered. I could tell that Mom suspected something was up, but I didn't let her pull it out of me until much later.

Even as I pushed to lift my skill level, my self-assurance sank—and not just because of the cruel comments. My coach and I were butting heads over which skills I should be learning. I wanted to learn more difficult routines with higher start values so that I could stay as competitive as possible; my coach thought I was asking for too much too soon—and he often told me so. Over time, I began to question my capabilities. *Does my coach think I'm talented enough to get to the highest levels of my sport?* Though I continued to train with him, I knew we weren't in step with each other.

So all in all, I went through a tough time at Excalibur. Were there plenty of coaches and gymnasts there who treated me with respect and love? Of course! And to this day, I appreciate that. I had some wonderful experiences there, I formed a few amazing friendships that I still cherish, and I improved as a gymnast. Yet that doesn't erase the sting of what I endured. Sometimes, the truth isn't one viewpoint versus another. It's both. In the end, I had some great days at Excalibur but I also faced some heartbreaking ones.

When I look back on it now, I realize I should've told Mom sooner about the comments about my nose and some of the other instances of bullying. If she'd known what I was experiencing, she could've handled the situation or even considered moving me to another gym. Even when you're scared—and I truly was!—it's always the right choice to speak up to an adult who really cares about you. For me, that person will always be Mom.

I ended my 2008 gymnastics season on a disappointing note. At the U.S. Classics—my first meet as a Junior International Elite gymnast—I came in tenth in all-around and eighth on uneven bars. Not my best meet. Then Mom and Arielle traveled all the way up to Boston to watch me compete in the Junior Visa Championship. I came in sixteenth place and didn't qualify for the national team. Ugh. Mom was there to comfort me afterward—but in her hotel room, not mine. The place where I was booked was $800 a night—so Mom, who barely had enough to even make the trip, booked the cheapest accommodations she could find. "There's always going to be another competition," Mom reassured me after the meet. "Take this as a learning experience and build on it. You're going to use this as your stepping stone to success."

The summer of 2008 brought a bright spot for me: the Beijing Olympics. When my siblings and I gathered around the set to watch the team finals that evening, the TV suddenly went off because of a storm.

When the screen went dark, I was like, *Are you kidding me?* "Mom, the power's out!" I yelled, praying I wouldn't miss a second of Shawn Johnson's upcoming performance on beam. I raced into my mother's room to ask her to check the circuit breaker and discovered Mom's TV was working just fine for some reason. So I jumped onto the bed and continued watching. My eyeballs were glued to the set. By this time, the dream I first had at age eight had blossomed into an unquenchable passion.

There was a lot to cheer about during those Olympic games. In the team finals we were trying to watch that night, the US women earned a silver medal behind China and in front of Romania. Then the women's team made history in the individual all-around competition a few days later when Nastia Liukin won the gold and Shawn Johnson seized the silver. The night that event aired, my family gathered at a friend's home for an Olympic viewing party. It was the first time the United States had claimed the top two medals for the same event. Yet it wasn't just the masterfully executed skills that caught my attention during the Beijing Olympics. It was one specific moment that happened on the sidelines.

For balance beam finals, both Shawn and Nastia had qualified, and Shawn took her spot on the balance beam early in the competition. Shawn's routine was awesome— from the full twisting back somersault and tuck back to the round-off with full twisting double back dismount. I was in awe of how she performed so well under pressure. Nothing seemed to get to her. When Shawn saw her score of 16.225, her face lit up—but would it be enough to keep her in the lead?

Later, Nastia's amazing beam routine brought her a score of 16.025. As graceful and powerful as Nastia's exercise was, her score was just shy of what she needed to land her on the top of the podium; she took the silver. When the final scoreboard showed Shawn's name in the number-one spot for beam finals, she and her coach embraced each other with a warmth and ease that made such an impression on me. That's the exact moment when I fell in love with Liang Chow, a man I'd never even met.

"That's my coach, Mom!" I announced. She just nodded and smiled with an expression that said, "Child, do you know that man lives on the other side of the country?" But I could feel it in my bones. Chow was the one.

"Stop playing inside this house." For months, my sister Arielle had repeated that sentence to Joyelle, John, and me—and for months, we hadn't listened to a word of it. "You're going to mess around and break something one day," she warned. We pretended to see her point, but the second she was out the door, the three of us went wild.

One afternoon while Mom and Arielle were away, we pulled out our giant, purplish-blue bouncy ball. "Let's play catch!" I said. I threw the ball at Joyelle; she caught it and hurled it over at John. Just as John was kicking the ball in my direction, the ball smashed right into our living room coffee table and made its legs wobble. And what was on top of that table? Arielle's most treasured possession—the multicolored pet fish she called Rainbow. "Oh my gosh!" the three of us shouted in unison. As the table tilted toward the floor, water from the small fish tank spread in every direction, all over our light-brown carpet. I raced over to the closet where Rainbow's quivering body had been thrown. John rushed over to the kitchen sink with the fish tank and refilled it with water, while Joy and I tried to scoop the wiggling fish into our palms.

"Hurry up, and put him back in the water!" I yelled. We did—just in time to keep him alive. We then thoroughly wiped down the carpet so that the huge water spot wouldn't be so noticeable.

Later that evening, Arielle came home to find the three of us lined up on the sofa, sitting perfectly still. "I see that I'm finally getting through to you about playing in this house," she said with a smirk. Seconds later, she walked over to the bowl and took a look at her fish. "What's *this*?" she said. A piece of brown carpet lint was stuck to Rainbow's tail. "Why is my fish so dirty?" I let out a little giggle but didn't say a word.

By night's end, our little secret became too much for us to bear, so we all filed into Arielle's room. "We have something to tell you," I said, looking down at the floor. "We're so sorry we almost killed Rainbow."

"I knew it!" said Arielle, who chuckled when we gave her all the details of the panicky scene. "This is why I kept telling y'all to stop playing in here!" And just like that, with a half smile, she let it go. That might've been a little easier to do since her fish was actually still alive, but hey, forgiveness is forgiveness, right? A big sister with an even bigger heart—I wish everyone in the world had one of those.

The Fishing Trip

My father loves to fish. One evening when I was thirteen, Dad took me, Joy, and John on a fishing trip near Chesapeake. The three of us cast our lines into the water and waited. John and Joy caught one fish. Then another. Then another. But after nearly an hour, I hadn't reeled in a single fish.

"Dad, I'm not catching anything," I said, fighting back tears.

"Let me see your rod," he said. He pulled it in and noticed something I'd clearly missed.

"There's no bait on the hook!" he said, chuckling. "How can you catch any fish without bait?" He then showed me how to attach my bait, and we cast my line back out into the water.

Within minutes, I was beside myself with excitement. "Dad," I said, "I caught my first fish, Dad!"

"That's great, Scooter," Dad said, beaming. "I'm proud of you."

How I longed to hear those very words in years already gone by— and in others to come.

Chapter Ten

Fractures well cured make us more strong.
—Ralph Waldo Emerson

Mom and I sat together in a booth in Ruby Tuesday's restaurant on Newtown Road and stared down at her phone on the tabletop. All day, we'd been expecting a call from my pediatrician, Dr. Robert Fink. Before the first ring was even complete, Mom picked up the cell and pressed the receiver to her ear. The way she furrowed her brow told me the news wasn't good.

After what seemed like forever, Mom thanked the doctor, hung up, and then looked straight at me without saying a word.

"Mom, what did the doctor say?"

Silence.

"Mom, what did he SAY?!" I pleaded.

More silence.

"Mom, please!"

She finally repeated the conversation for me. "I'm

so sorry," he'd said, "but there is no way Gabrielle can compete at her upcoming meet. She will be out for a while." He referred Mom to an orthopedic surgeon for follow-up care.

I bawled. "But what about my competitions?" I shrieked between sobs. "I can't be away for ten whole weeks!" The U.S. Classics were less than a month away, and that competition would be followed by one of the biggest of my career—the Junior Olympic National Championships in August 2009. I was devastated by the thought of sitting on the sidelines—yet even scarier was the possibility of ending my entire career.

When my mother heard the results, she was livid. Injuries happen a lot in my sport—but Mom knew it was my coach's job to make sure I wasn't hurting myself by training too much. Mom also knew just how strongly I'd been bitten by the Olympic bug—and the upcoming National Championship was an important step along the path to that dream. "I'm so sorry, Brie," Mom said as tears threatened to overflow her lower lids. We both then held onto each other in that restaurant and cried our eyes out. Mom rubbed my back as I sobbed into her shirt sleeve, but I was inconsolable. "You want the chocolate brownie sundae you ordered?" the waiter asked, with a look on his face that said, "I know I'm interrupting something important." I shook my head no. Neither of us was in the mood for chocolate after all.

When we visited the orthopedic surgeon, the news got worse. "It looks like Gabrielle has a stress fracture in a growth plate in her wrist," the surgeon said. "It's the result of overtraining and overuse. If she doesn't stop training for at least ten weeks, she'll risk a permanent injury that could end her career."

I'd first felt the pain in my wrist a week earlier, and I had prayed that it would just go away on its own. When it didn't, I told Mom, who immediately scheduled an appointment with my pediatrician. *It couldn't be that bad*, I thought as the doctor took the X-rays. *It's probably just a minor sprain.* Clearly, I'd been wrong.

That weekend, I moped around the house in my PJs. Mom and my coach made the final decision: I wouldn't compete in the U.S. Classics in July. It just wasn't worth the risk of further injuring my wrist and putting my career in jeopardy. So even when I did go to the gym, all I could do was conditioning and legwork—skills that didn't require the use of my wrist.

"What about the National Championship in August? Is there any chance I'll be healed by then?" I asked my mother.

Mom paused before she gave me her answer. "Brie Baby," she said, "I don't know. We'll just have to wait and see."

Eight and a half weeks into my recovery time from the stress fracture, my wrist began feeling better—much better. But my orthopedic surgeon didn't want to hear a peep about me competing. "Give yourself time to heal," he insisted. "You're not ready." But he agreed to do another test anyway to check on my progress.

What the surgeon discovered astounded even him. When he compared the X-ray of my fractured wrist with the X-ray of my healthy wrist, he couldn't even tell which one had been injured! "I still want you to be careful," he warned. "Work your way back into training slowly." Those are the words he said, but what I heard was, "You can compete in the National Championship."

So the following day, I began training again on beam. I also practiced some modified floor routines—but I stayed away from the vault and bar. Even though I'd had very minimal training once the championship rolled around, Coach Gustavo decided to let me compete on floor and beam.

Day one of the meet was a disaster; during my first tumbling pass on my floor routine, I crashed terribly. "I don't think I was prepared enough," I told Mom afterward. She agreed, and so did my coach—which is why I opted out of my floor exercise on the second day of competition. My balance beam routine gave me a chance to redeem myself—but after a falter, the best I could pull off was fifth place.

———

The first time I tasted a funnel cake, I was smitten. When Arielle, Joyelle, John, and I were small, Mom used to take us to the Busch Gardens amusement park in Williamsburg, Virginia, a place where funnel cake stands abounded. I can practically still smell the aroma of the warm, round pieces of golden dough, sprinkled with powdered sugar and extra crispy around the edges. Joyelle and I were hooked.

"Mom, can you make us some funnel cakes?" we'd ask every few months. "Maybe some other time," she always answered. But "some other time" never seemed to roll around, even though we found a recipe online and printed it out for her. So late one night, when Joy and I were craving a funnel cake, we got a bright idea: we'd sneak into the kitchen to make our own.

Mom didn't like us to use the stove—especially when she wasn't there to oversee us. But since it was nearly midnight, Mom was fast asleep. We slid out of bed, found the recipe we'd printed, and tiptoed into the kitchen. In the dark, we gathered the ingredients on the countertop. Flour? Check. Milk and eggs? Double check. Sugar, vegetable oil, and vanilla extract? Triple check.

"Did you see that?" Joyelle said.

"Did I see *what*?" I whispered back.

"It's a spider!" Joyelle flipped on the lights as we both tried to squelch our shrieks so we wouldn't awaken Mom. Since my sister was the older, braver one, she grabbed an old shoe that was sitting at the front doorway and hit the black spider with it. "I got him!" she said. We then went back to work on our project—this time, with the lights on.

Joyelle measured out each of our ingredients and poured them into the big bowl I was holding. Using a wooden spoon, she mixed everything together. With each stir, the thick mix began looking a lot less like cake batter—and a lot more like bread dough.

"I think we did something wrong," I told Joyelle. As we glanced back over the recipe, the mistake popped out at us: Joyelle had put in two *cups* of sugar instead of two *tablespoons* of sugar.

"Let's just double it," Joyelle said. I nodded in agreement.

In less than a minute, it became clear that we hadn't fixed our mess—we'd multiplied it. Our bowl overflowed with a big, sugary mass of dough! But since we'd already gotten this far, we figured we might as well take the last step: frying up the batter. I turned on the electric stove while Joyelle tilted the bottle of cooking oil toward the skillet and poured.

"Do you think that's enough?" she asked.

"That looks about right," I answered. We let the oil heat up for about five minutes until it started to form bubbles. Perfect. We then pulled a small piece of dough off the glob and formed a thin, round cake. I placed it into the oil.

What happened next? Not much. After the heavy dough sank to the bottom of the skillet, it just lay there and soaked up the oil.

"Should the oil be hotter?" Joy finally asked.

Bingo—so I turned up the knob on the stove. Three minutes later, we didn't have a funnel cake—but we did have some kind of deformed pancake!

"We really screwed this up!" Joyelle whispered.

Before escaping back to bed, we did away with our evidence. Joyelle wiped down the counter and stovetop, while I put away the remaining ingredients and quietly washed our dishes. And what did we do with the mass of leftover dough? We dropped it into a big plastic bag and put it at the bottom of the trashcan. After one final look around the kitchen, we tiptoed back to our room.

Mom never found out about our funnel cake fiasco—or at least Joyelle and I don't think she did. Our mother has a funny way of acting like she doesn't notice something—but then five years later, we discover that she was on to us all along!

Later that same year, Mom got sick. Extremely sick. She became ill after she took some prescription medication. Her adverse reaction to that medication was so severe that my sisters, brother, and I were sure we would lose her.

"The doctors are putting me on a medical leave from my job," Mom told us one evening when she'd gathered us in her bedroom. "I just need some time to recover." Her condition wasn't life threatening, but she was in so much pain that she certainly felt like she was near death—and we thought so too. To this day, I have never been more scared.

The following months were not only an emotional roller coaster, they became a financial one. When Mom began her medical leave, it took three months for her to receive disability pay. For the first month, we lived on the little savings Mom had socked away in the bank. "God will provide," she assured us, but we could tell that even she was a little nervous about how we would survive.

Back in 2006, after my parents separated, our mother began receiving steady child support payments from my father, who went on active military duty for a time. But when those payments suddenly stopped without a warning a year and a half later, we were back to praying our way from one paycheck to the next. When Mom got down to the last $3 in her checking account, she knew she had to do something drastic. So she pulled out the most valuable piece of jewelry she'd ever owned, a half-carat diamond ring in a custom setting, and took it down to the pawn shop. Once there, she slowly opened the door, made her way to the counter, and set out the ring. "How much can I get for this?" she asked. The store owner picked up the ring and examined it before he finally gave her an estimate: $750. That was barely enough to get us through the second month of Mom's medical leave.

By the third month, our situation had grown worse. We literally had no money for groceries. Our last gallon of milk sat nearly empty in the fridge next to a half carton of eggs. Our mother—a proud woman who has always worked so tirelessly to provide for us—has a very hard time asking for help. But this time, we were desperate for it.

"I had either sold or pawned every possession of value that we had, and there was just no money left," she recalls of that time. "That's when I knew I had to do the one thing that I have never ever wanted to do: I had to go on food stamps." So one morning, Mom gathered up all the strength she could muster to lift herself out of bed, get dressed, and drive down to the Social Services office on Virginia Beach Boulevard. "I cried so many tears because I couldn't believe I'd found myself in this predicament," she says. "But I did what I had to do to make sure my children could eat." That month and for dozens of others to follow, we did eat—but only by the grace of God.

Even while Mom was on medical leave, she scrambled to keep money flowing. A friend told her about a slimming body garment called "Body Magic," an item Mom could sell online. "It'll produce immediate revenue," the friend assured her, "because everyone wants to look good in their clothes." When Mom got her own garment in the mail, she tried it on—and it took all four of us kids to help her get into that thing! John wasn't happy at all about having to fasten the hooks on the front of the slimmer. "Men aren't supposed to be doing this sort of thing, Mom!" he joked. But Mom was desperate enough to try anything. Once she was convinced that this was a legitimate business opportunity involving a product that worked as advertised, she began selling the garments. She used that income to keep the utilities paid—but she didn't have enough to cover the mortgage.

Many years ago, food stamps were actual stamps, but they've since been replaced by a debit-like card. Each time we went to the grocery store, my mother felt ashamed to pull out that card. We once ran into one of Mom's former coworkers—and Mom was so afraid that woman would spot the card that she actually got out of line. "You can go ahead of us," she told the woman. "We forgot something."

Our mother then pushed the cart to the back of the store and pretended she was getting some orange juice. In the meantime, my siblings and I secretly checked to see if the woman had left the store. "Is she gone yet?" Mom asked. When the woman finally rolled her grocery cart out the front door, we returned to the line. Even still, Mom looked around slowly before she pulled out the card. The debit card had just enough on it to cover the milk and bread— but never enough to erase Mom's feeling of humiliation.

Over the following months and years, Mom's physical condition grew better. And better. And better. After the physicians took her off of the medication that had made her so sick, they eventually found the right prescription. And though we still lived awfully close to a financial cliff's edge, we did what we could to cut corners on costs—and to cut coupons out of the weekly newspaper.

A fractured wrist. An ill mother. A funnel cake in the bottom of the trash can. Where could I go from there? Good thing I serve a God who specializes in making broken things whole again.

The Ice Cream

Once my father was home from Iraq, he'd pop up to see me from time to time, usually when I least expected it. In 2010, when I competed in the Excalibur Cup, that's exactly what happened. I hadn't even talked to him for weeks—then, suddenly, while I was on the competition floor, I looked up to see him smiling and waving in the audience. Afterward, he came up to hug me. "Hi, Scooter," he said. He'd started calling me that because when I first began crawling, I'd scooted around on both knees before I learned to put one knee in front of the other. "Hi, Dad," I answered flatly.

We never talked about the tough subjects, like why he and my mother had split or when I'd see him next. Instead, we did a lot of small talking, about things like movies or puppies. It was complicated, because I had such mixed emotions toward him. On one hand, I was excited when I did see him; on the other hand, I was disappointed that he was seldom around. Mom constantly encouraged Dad to be in my life, as well as in the lives of Joy and John, and she often told him when I had big meets coming up. But he seldom showed up for anything— and when he did, as in the day he dropped by the Excalibur Cup, it felt awkward for me.

Sometimes, Mom would arrange for Dad to pick me up after training if she had to stay late at work. On one afternoon when my father was supposed to pick me up at five o'clock, Dad first stopped to buy a Christmas tree to go in the home he shared with his new girlfriend. He pulled up at seven thirty. "We'll go get ice cream if you don't tell your mom I was late to get you," he bribed. I nodded, and we stopped at Dairy Queen. Later, Mom indeed asked him why I was so late. "Oh, we picked up ice cream on the way home, and Brie helped me Christmas shop," he fibbed. Tightening my grip around my cup, I stepped aside and spooned up the rest of my ice cream in silence.

Chapter Eleven

*Twenty years from now, you will be more
disappointed by the things that you didn't do than
by the ones you did do.*

—MARK TWAIN

"LIANG CHOW IS COMING TO EXCALIBUR." WHEN ONE OF MY COACHES
uttered that sentence, I froze. "Do you mean Liang Chow—
Shawn Johnson's coach?" I finally managed to ask.

"That's right," my coach said. "He and some other
trainers will be here to teach a clinic next week." I could
have fainted.

Since that moment during the 2008 Beijing Olympics,
when I'd seen Liang Chow and Shawn Johnson embrace
after her beam final, I'd thought of him constantly. And
every few weeks, I brought him up to my mother with the
same refrain: "That's my coach." We both knew that the
chances of me even meeting Liang Chow hovered around
zero; he happened to live 1,200 miles away in Iowa. So on

that afternoon in July 2010, when I heard he was actually coming to my gym in Virginia Beach, I flipped out.

On the day of the clinic, I came into the gym and spotted Liang Chow right away. My heartbeat doubled in speed. *There he is!* I thought. Later, my teammates and I introduced ourselves to him. "I'm Gabrielle Douglas," I announced as confidently as I could. He smiled and nodded before moving on to the next girl.

Once the introductions were complete, he gave us a warm-up: five sprints on the runway. We then began working on skills. When I showed him my double twist on vault, Chow said, "Whoa! That was powerful. Do you compete with the two-and-a-half twist on vault?" When I told him I didn't, he was surprised. "On the next one, try a double twist. Then when you land, jump and do a half turn." I nodded then did exactly what he told me to do.

"Okay, now do a two and a half—and we'll take the mat out and have you land in the foam squishy pit." When I did the exercise and landed in the pit, Chow was again impressed. "You can easily do it on the mat!" he said. He walked over and put in the mat for me. And just like that, after one session with Chow, I went from performing a double-twisting vault to executing one of the most difficult vaults in gymnastics, the Amanar. That's when it clicked in my head: if he could teach me a two-and-a-half in one day, what other big skills could he teach me?

Before I left the gym, I asked Chow if I could have a photo taken with him. "Sure," he said. Mom was there at the gym that afternoon, and she snapped the picture for us. My coach had asked Mom to take Chow to the airport (his original ride fell through), so he and Mom chatted on the way. Mom told Chow how pleased she was that he had taught me the Amanar vault. She thanked him again as she dropped him off.

I cherished my photo. Each time I looked down at it during the following days, I visualized Chow as my coach—the one who could take me to the next level of gymnastics. That's when I began plotting.

My grandmother, Miss Carolyn, calls her mother Boo, which is short for Beulah. The rest of us simply call her Grandmother, even though she's really our great-grandma. On either Thanksgiving or Christmas, my family would visit Grandmother in Gary, Indiana. That meant every fall, I began counting the days until we could head to her house—especially since that involved one of my favorite desserts.

"How do you always get the crust so perfectly golden brown?" I asked Grandmother. We usually arrived to the smell of her best recipe: homemade sweet-potato pie. The fresh sweet potatoes, cinnamon, brown sugar, and creamy butter had swirled together to fill her living room with an amazing aroma. "The recipe is my little secret!" Grandmother would always tease. I could hardly wait to taste that pie, which she kept wrapped and on her countertop. Even now, just the thought of that pie makes me want a huge slice.

Miss Carolyn raised my mother in Gary during the first three years of Mom's life; my grandparents divorced when my mother was small. After Mom's parents separated, Mom spent summers and every other major holiday with her father in Gary. My mother has one sister, Bianca, who is eleven years younger than Mom and born on the same day, February 16. (We've always called my mother's sister "Tia"—she was once taking Spanish classes and loved the way that sounded.) When Mom was a girl, Miss Carolyn even put Tia into a recreational gymnastics class for a little while. That happened back during the Mary Lou Retton era, when families around the country had watched Mary win gold at the 1984 Olympics. My grandmother has always been a very cultured woman, and she worked hard to give her children everything that she could. After she and my grandfather separated and eventually divorced, she joined the Navy; Mom, then just four, lived with her grandmother in Gary; at five, Miss Carolyn moved her to Norfolk, where she was stationed.

Miss Carolyn wasn't wealthy, yet she valued education so much that she scraped together enough to send her children to private school. When all the homework was finished, Miss Carolyn would call her girls into the living room to watch things like figure skating and gymnastics on television. "Look how disciplined you have to be to master all four of these apparatuses," she would explain. She wanted to expose them to as much of the world as she could; that was her way of giving them a vision for what was possible in their hometown and far beyond it.

I loved having Miss Carolyn close by in Virginia—especially when it was my birthday, lol! She always made a big deal about my and my siblings' birthdays, especially since we are her only grandchildren. The year I turned fourteen, she picked me up and took me to the Cheesecake Factory. She always lets me choose the activity and restaurant on my birthday, as she does when she celebrates the birthdays of my sisters and brother.

"What would you like to order, Brie?" she asked. I straightened my back and shoulders and flipped through the enormous menu.

"I'll have the macaroni and cheese balls," I finally announced. We laughed our way through dinner before Miss Carolyn pulled out the gift she'd brought for me, a bag filled with nail polish and headbands. By age twelve, I'd started to set aside my tomboy ways (thanks to the influence of my sister, Joyelle, who always picks out the cutest girlie outfits!). So when I opened the gift, my huge smile showed just how pleased I was. "Thanks, Miss Carolyn!" I said, giving her a big hug. As we left the restaurant and walked out to the car, I began looking ahead to the next birthday—that one time of year when I could always be sure I'd have Miss Carolyn all to myself.

"If I'm going to make it to the Olympics, I need better coaching." Mom had just picked me up from my double session at Excalibur, and we'd arrived back at our town house. In the two days since I'd met Chow at that clinic,

I'd become obsessed with a single thought—I wanted him to coach me. That's what led me to make my declaration to Mom that afternoon: "I want to move to Iowa and train with Liang Chow."

"Brie, have you lost your mind?" my mother said, widening her pupils and raising her voice by an octave with each word. "Chow lives in West Des Moines, Iowa. Have you looked at a map lately? Iowa is nowhere *close* to Virginia Beach! There's no way I'm sending my baby across the country. You just need to make the best of your training here."

It's not that I wasn't making some progress at Excalibur. I was. But that progress simply wasn't happening fast enough. For months, I'd been struggling with an uneven bar skill called the Pak salto, a move in which you release the high bar and then do a backward flip before catching the low bar. While doing the skill, I'd often hit my feet on the floor—and that's a major score deduction of five-tenths of a point. The fact that I hadn't yet mastered the Pak salto had kept me from medaling in all-around competitions; I'd often end up in fourth place rather than on the podium. I'm sure my coach was doing his best to teach me the skill, but his technique wasn't working for me. Plus, we hadn't been working to upgrade my other skills; after that one session with Chow, I hadn't even been able to continue doing the vault he taught me. I kept thinking, *How can I compete if I have no big skills in my routines?* With the 2012 Olympics just two short years away, I knew I had to do something—and fast.

Mom wanted me to succeed; she just wanted me to do it a lot closer to home.

"I've got to train with a coach who can take me to the next level—and that's Coach Chow," I said.

"If they don't teach you anything for the next few months," she said, "I will think about moving you."

"But there's no time to think about it!" I pressed. "If I don't move now, I won't be good enough by 2012. And if I do go to the Olympics, I want to do it big!" I knew I'd crossed the line by raising my voice to Mom. But in that moment, all I cared about was one thing—my Olympic dream. And if I couldn't get Mom to see my point, that dream might be out of reach forever. "If I don't change coaches," I told her, "I'm quitting." I then stormed out of the living room, stomped into my bedroom, and yanked the door closed. That's how my July ended.

Chapter Twelve

When I let go of what I am,
I become what I might be.
When I let go of what I have,
I receive what I need.

—The Tao Te Ching, ancient Chinese text

In August, I did a lot of sulking. Mom would barely even discuss my idea of moving to Iowa to train with Chow. So I tried another approach: rounding up reinforcements. One evening, I huddled with my two sisters and told them just how passionate I was about this idea. "If I don't make this move," I explained, "I may never get to the Olympics." They immediately got it. "I need you to help me out with this," I told them. "We all have to persuade Mom."

Arielle—the sibling who has the best track record for getting through to our mother—made a list of pros and cons. She and Joyelle then presented that list to Mom one evening when our mother was already in a fairly good mood. "On the plus side," Arielle explained, "Brie might get a coach she can bond with. Her confidence level would increase. Her skill level would improve, making her more competitive among elite gymnasts. And Brie might also make it all the way to London and get the gold." She paused before continuing. "Of course, there is one huge con—we'd all miss her so much."

"But *pleeeease*, Mom," Joy added, "you just have to let her go. There's no other way she'll make it to the Olympics."

John was the one voice of dissent—he couldn't see Mom sending his sidekick and baby sister to another state. "If you send her to Iowa," he said, "how will I be able to protect her all the way from Virginia?!"

Mom didn't say too much after my sisters made their case. But she also didn't say no, and as far as I was concerned, that was major progress. After Arielle and Joy had pleaded with Mom in a series of follow-up conversations, I could tell something had clicked. Mom was actually starting to change her mind.

Kaiya and I will always be friends—but when she left Excalibur in 2009, we missed seeing each other at the gym for so many hours every week. Once Kaiya moved on, I formed an even tighter bond with another amazing friend. Her name is Beka.

Beka and I did just about everything together—both inside the gym and away from it. I sometimes even spent the night at her house. On double-session days, my mother and Beka's mother took turns picking up both of us. On Mom's days, she often took us to play at a little park behind Kempsville Library once our homework was done. After gym, we loved snacking on Hot Pockets and peaches. Then if we were at Beka's house, we'd create our own obstacle course in her backyard. On the days when I was staying at Beka's house for a sleepover, we'd put on our Heelys (those shoes with the wheels embedded into the soles) and roller skate all over the neighborhood.

One Fourth of July weekend, I spent a night at Beka's house. We awakened to the smell of hot, buttery cinnamon rolls; Beka's dad had gotten up early to make a fresh batch. "Help yourselves to breakfast, girls!" he said as we followed the mouth-watering aroma right into the kitchen. We didn't have gym that day, so once we'd devoured our rolls, we decided to create our own little workout.

"How about if we do some jump rope?" I said, grabbing on to both handles of the rope. Beka grabbed another jump rope, and we began jumping and counting in unison: "One, two, three ..." After we'd completed a couple dozen jumps with lots of giggling in between, we decided to pull out the bikes for a ride.

"Here, you can use this bike," Beka offered. Before I mounted the bike, I noticed my shoelace was untied—but in our excitement to get rolling, I didn't stop to retie my shoe. Big mistake! By the time we got halfway down the street, my lace had wrapped all the way around the pedal.

"Hey, wait — my foot's gonna get caught in the

spokes!" I yelled out to Beka, who was pedaling beside me. I was so worried about untangling my shoelace from the pedal that I hardly noticed that I was drifting to the right, onto the road. Then just when I looked up again—*bam*! I ran right into the back of a parked truck.

Beka panicked. She slammed on her brakes and ran to my side. "Are you okay, Gabby?" she said. I could see drops of blood falling from my face to the ground. I had broken my two front teeth in half.

Beka started crying when I took my hands away from my face to show her the damage. "Oh, no!" she screamed, "I'm so sorry, Gabby!" We hurried back to the house, and Beka's dad called my mother immediately. Mom made an emergency dentist appointment for me. The good news is that both teeth broke right beneath the nerve, which means I didn't need implants or crown work. So my careless mistake cost me two broken teeth—but you want to hear something crazy? I was even more disappointed that I had to miss two whole days of training. That's just how sore and swollen my mouth was. What a pain!

I suited up in my hot-pink leo for a big competition: the U.S. Junior National Championships. In August 2010, Mom traveled with me to Hartford, Connecticut, so she could watch me perform. I earned a silver on the balance beam, I claimed the eighth spot on the floor exercise, and I grabbed fourth place in the individual all-around. After the meet, my coach stopped in at the hotel room.

Mom, Arie, Joy, and John—who'd all stayed at another hotel—were already there with me, catching up after the competition.

"I can't believe you did so good," my coach said when he came in. "I thought you might be ninth or tenth in the all-around—but never fourth." I couldn't believe what I'd just heard—and neither could Mom.

After the coach left the room, I plopped down on my bed and turned to my mother. "You see, if my coach doesn't have faith in me," I said, "how can I have faith in myself?" That was Mom's second aha moment: even if she didn't send me all the way to Iowa like my sisters and I had pleaded, she needed to find me a different coach. What happened over the next four weeks is nothing short of a miracle.

Placing fourth at the Junior National Championship was enough to put me on the Junior National Team for the first time. That gave me the chance to compete at the upcoming Pan American Championships in Guadalajara, Mexico. First, the not-so-good news: I fell twice on the beam, and that knocked me out of all-around placement. And now for some much better news: in addition to helping the team score gold, I won first place in uneven bars—my first international gold medal. That's mostly because my main coach, who was traveling in the weeks leading up to the Pan Am meet, had finally allowed another coach at the gym to train me. That coach's training technique had made all the difference in my bar routine—yet my primary coach wouldn't hand me off to anyone else at the gym. So if I wanted to get better, I had one option: I had to move on. After Guadalajara, Mom was as convinced of that as I was.

At first, Mom considered moving our whole family to Texas so that I could be trained by a well-known coach there. "I have family in Dallas," Mom said, "so maybe that's an option."

When Texas didn't work out, Mom finally picked up her phone and called Liang Chow. He remembered her from that clinic at Excalibur, especially since she'd driven him to the airport afterward.

"Gabrielle would like to train with you," Mom explained once she got Chow on the line.

He paused. "I've got to think about whether to take her," he finally said, explaining that he didn't encourage gymnasts to jump from gym to gym. "It might be too late to change coaches so close to the Olympic games—and I don't know if I have enough time to get her ready."

"But she's convinced you are the only one who can train her," Mom responded. "Is there any way you can take her?"

Chow hesitated again. "Well, my position as a coach is to help kids achieve their dreams," he continued. "If a gymnast wants to reach for higher possibilities, like Gabby does, then I think it's fair for me to at least take a look at her. Let's schedule a one-week trial for Gabrielle in Iowa."

I was ecstatic. That same day, Mom and I began making preparations to fly to West Des Moines. In the meantime, Chow called a high-level staff member at USA

Gymnastics to talk through the possibility of coaching me. "You have to train this kid," the USAG member told Chow. "Team USA needs her." So before Mom and I could even pack our dental floss, the phone rang. It was Chow. "I will take her," he announced. And those were the four little words that changed my life forever.

Chapter Thirteen

You can never cross the ocean unless you have the
courage to lose sight of the shore.
—Christopher Columbus

I KNOW WHAT TO PACK FOR A WEEKEND — BUT WHAT IN THE WORLD DO
you pack for a two-year journey that might end at the
London Olympics? I stood over the huge black suitcase
in my bedroom with most of my must-take possessions
in a big pile. I'd gathered everything from my passport
and my grips to my team gear. "I wish I had a camera," I
told Joy, who laid on her bed and watched me pack in the
middle of the floor. "I'll just take pictures on my phone
and send them to you."

Mom and I visited a couple discount department
stores where I could find a few items to take with me. As
for shoes, I bought a pair of brown boots and Vans in
a variety of colors—gray and purple, blue, and black. I
got my first pair of heels—make that black-velvet *kitten*
heels, thank you!—in case I ever needed to dress up.

Mom also bought me jeggings (a cross between jeans and leggings, for the uninitiated), a few cute tops to wear with them, some jogging suits—and, of course, a long, heavy coat. I'd definitely need that in Iowa, where temperatures can dip far below freezing during winter. By this time, I'd made the full transformation from tomboy to fashionista—and though we didn't have much money to spend, I wanted to show up stylish. Mom agreed. "You need to go out looking good or don't go out at all!" she'd often joke.

The plan was for Mom and me to fly together to West Des Moines. She'd stay with me for two weeks to help me transition, and Arielle, who couldn't change her work schedule to take the whole trip, would join us for the second week. Arielle knew Mom would need her on the flight back home, because leaving me in Iowa (when she barely even let her children spend the night away from home!) was almost more than she could bear.

How I wished they could stay beside me for a month, a year ... a lifetime! At one point, Arielle had actually considered going with me to live in Iowa—the two of us would get an apartment, and she'd work while I trained. But money was still tight, so my sister thought it was best to stay in Virginia and avoid any additional financial burdens. Plus Mom had arranged for me to reside with a host family—a group of strangers in a city I'd never even thought about visiting, much less calling home.

Top: Gabrielle started formal gymnastics in 2002 at age 6. This photo was taken in 2004, the year she went on to become the Virginia State Champion.

Bottom: The girls take some time to goof off!

Photo courtesy of Natalie Hawkins

Top: Gabrielle shows grace and beauty during her floor routine at the 2006 US Classic.

Bottom: Gabrielle on the balance beam during practice at the 2012 AT&T American Cup at Madison Square Garden.

Timothy A. Clary/AFP/Getty Images

This aerial view shows Gabrielle's perfect form on the balance beam during the women's Olympic gymnastics trials. Gabrielle won the Olympic trials, which earned her the only guaranteed spot on the team.

AP Images/Julie Jacobson

Top: Nicknamed "Flying Squirrel" for her amazing aerial skills on the uneven bars, Gabrielle competes here during day one of the 2012 Visa Championships.

Bottom: Gabrielle competes on the vault in the Individual All-Around final of the London 2012 Olympic Games.

Left: Julian Finney/Getty Images. Inset: Christopher Hanewinckel/USA Today Sports

Above: Coach Liang Chow hugs Gabrielle after her performance in the floor exercise in the Women's Individual All-Around final.

Right: Gabrielle celebrates on the podium after winning the gold medal in the Artistic Gymnastics Women's Individual All-Around final.

Ben Stansall/AFP/Getty Images

Mike Coppola/Getty Images

Top left: Gabrielle, Mckayla Maroney, Alexandra Raisman, and Kyla Ross celebrate winning team gold in the 2012 Summer Olympics.

Top right: Gabrielle and her mom pose for a picture at Citi Field in New York City.

Bottom: Gabrielle, right, hugs her aunt, Bianca Williams, after she arrives at the Norfolk (VA) International Airport on Thursday, Aug. 16, 2012, for a visit to her home in Virginia Beach, VA. At far left is Douglas's sister, Arielle Hawkins, brother, John Douglas, left, and her uncle, David Jemmott, right.

AP Images/Virginian-Pilot, Ross Taylor

Top: Gabrielle with the Partons—her host family in West Des Moines, Iowa.

Bottom left: Travis Parton hugs Gabrielle immediately after she wins her individual gold medal.

Bottom right: Gabrielle attends the 'America's Got Talent' post show red carpet at New Jersey Performing Arts Center August 15, 2012.

Top: First Lady Michelle Obama and Gabrielle chat during an interview with host Jay Leno in August 2012.

Bottom: Gabrielle and her teammates Kyla Ross, Jordyn Wieber, Aly Raisman, and McKayla Maroney are interviewed by Bob Costas after winning team gold.

A few months before I left for Iowa, it was spring break—which meant that I had a rare week off from both school and the gym. So John and I pulled out our bikes (mine was pink) and pedaled around the neighborhood. After a couple days of rolling around, I was so bored. "Man, I wish a dog would come chase us," I joked. I made this comment at least twice a day for the next two days.

True story: On the final day of our spring break, a pit bull came out of nowhere and bounded toward us. "Aaaagh!" I screamed.

In an instant, John and I stood up on our bikes and pedaled as fast and as hard as we could.

"He's gaining on us!" John yelled, with sweat forming on his forehead. A moment later, the pit bull got close enough to rip off my left blue Nike with his teeth. I panicked and tried to keep pedaling.

"Go faster!" John shouted. But I couldn't, because we'd rolled right onto a grassy area where our wheels wouldn't rotate as quickly unless I shifted gears. I kid you not: just as the pit bull was raising up on his back legs to leap up onto me, a guardian angel appeared—in the form of another dog! When the pit bull heard his fellow canine barking, he got distracted, turned away from me, and raced toward the other dog, which was inside a gated yard. But before we could race home on our bikes, can you believe that dog came after us again?

"He's still chasing us, John!" I shouted. Just as the pit bull was crossing the street in our direction, our second angel came to the rescue—a red Toyota sedan backed up into the pit bull. The dog didn't die, but he began limping enough to allow my brother and me time to get home. John was like, "Go, go, go, go—pick it up, Brie!" Once we were inside our gate, we shut it and raced into the town house. So scary!

Someone wise once said this: "Be careful what you ask for—you just might get it." And whether you're requesting a dog-chasing adventure or a trip to the other side of the country, here's what I can tell you for sure: Asking is one thing. Getting is another.

On my last day at Excalibur, Mom told my coach that I was moving on—by then, she'd already had three meetings to discuss the possibility of my departure. Mom again explained what we'd all known for months: I needed different coaching in order to lift my skills to the next level. I cleaned out my locker and hugged some of my teammates. A few of us cried together. Even though it was sad to say good-bye to my friends, I knew there were exciting days to come. When I walked out the front door of Excalibur for the final time, I never looked back— mostly because there was far too much to see, do, and experience just over the horizon.

The last item I threw in my suitcase was my blue-and-white stuffed whale, Willy. On my fourteenth birthday, after eating at the Cheesecake Factory, Miss Carolyn and I went shopping at Kohl's. I spotted Willy on the sales rack.

"Do you want him?" Miss Carolyn asked. I looked

over at Willy's big head, his huge eyes with those adorable eyelashes, and there was only one answer I could give—an emphatic yes. Since that day, Willy's soft, furry body has been right next to me on my bed and with me at every national camp. So I wouldn't even dream of going all the way to Iowa without him. I placed him on top of the other belongings in my suitcase and zipped the bag all the way around.

One giant suitcase and one big backpack—that's all I took. "If you need something from Virginia," Mom said, "I can ship it to you." I wondered, *Is it possible to ship a mother, three siblings, and two dogs to Iowa?*

A few days before my departure, my father's family hosted a small good-bye party for me—Mom had told my dad I was moving to Iowa. Then on the evening before my flight, I said my good-byes to Joyelle and John, since I knew they'd be sleeping when we arose for our six o'clock flight the next morning. We didn't talk too much about the separation to come; it hadn't quite hit us just how long our months apart would feel. So that evening, we just hugged and whispered a few rounds of I miss you's and I love you's before we all went to bed.

The next morning, as Mom loaded the car with our suitcases, my dog sat in the living room. "Bye, Zoway," I said before I closed the door. A moment later, I reopened the door. "Bye, Zoway," I said again louder, as if it hadn't registered with him first time around. Zoway just looked at me like, "Would you please just go ahead and leave already?"

Later, on the way to the airport, I told my mother, "Zoway is going to forget me."

"Will you stop it?" Mom said. "Dogs have really good memories. Zoway will always know who you are." More than two years and one extraordinary adventure later, I'd finally return home to discover for myself Mom was right.

Chapter Fourteen

And we know that all things work together
for good to those who love God, to those who are
the called according to His purpose.
—ROMANS 8:28, NKJV

ON THE SEPTEMBER 2010 AFTERNOON MOM AND I ARRIVED AT CHOW'S
Gymnastics & Dance Institute in West Des Moines,
I came ready to sweat. "I want to take you through a
normal four-hour session," Chow had told me beforehand by phone. "That way, I can get a feel for where you
are." And what was a "normal" session at Chow's gym?
A whole-body workout that included thirty minutes of
conditioning, followed by a sequential rotation on vault,
bars, beam, and floor. We ended with about twenty
minutes of conditioning and flexibility exercises.

After the session, Chow sat down to chat with Mom
and me. "My dream is to get to the Olympics," I stated
with confidence while a drop of sweat made its way down
my back.

Chow paused. "Well, you haven't given me much time," he finally said. "Your difficulty level and physical condition need a lot of upgrading. I don't know how hard you're willing to work—but there is a lot of work to be done."

He paused again, just long enough for me to interject. "I will give you one hundred percent every day," I told Chow, looking directly into his eyes.

Chow cleared his throat. "I'll be very straight with you," he said. "I see the possibility for you to go to the Olympics, but I cannot guarantee it will happen. What I can promise you is this: I'll do my best to get you ready."

When it came to training, Chow took a less-is-more approach: I only had twenty-eight hours of sessions each week, versus thirty-six at my previous gym. Why might fewer hours bring a stronger result? Because the twenty-eight hours were more intently focused on skill building—we did no less than fifteen routines each day. "Every coach has his or her own methods," Chow would often remind me, "and one approach isn't necessarily right or wrong. It's about choosing an approach that works best to prepare a particular gymnast." In my case, Chow's approach was a winner.

Long before Chow was a coach, he was a gymnast. As a child in Beijing, China, Chow began his training at age five, after he was chosen by his district club because his tumbling skills showed promise. For many years, he competed on the men's Chinese national team, where he won the World Cup National Championships in 1990.

Chow then relocated to the United States with his wife, Liwen. (PS: Everyone calls her Li for short.) Moving to America was his aunt's idea: She was already here, completing her Ph.D. at the University of Iowa in Des Moines. When Chow arrived with very little English under his belt, he took the one job he knew he could excel at: assistant gymnastics coach for the men's program at the University of Iowa. When five of his students made the national team, Chow was asked to take on the women's team. He did — but, over time, he realized he could coach his students even better if he started with them when they were younger. That's why Chow and Li eventually opened their own training center in 1998. Within five years, business was booming enough for him to build a second facility on his eleven acres of land. The youngest gymnasts he trains usually gather in the new building; the older girls meet in the original building. That's the building where Chow and I had our first official training session in fall 2010.

That's also where I met Shawn Johnson, the Olympic champion whose interactions with Chow at the Beijing Olympics had eventually led me to Des Moines. Back when I arrived, Shawn was still training hard to make an Olympic comeback — a knee injury eventually put that dream out of reach.

"Hello, Gabrielle," she said with a smile, extending her hand when I arrived at Chow's gym. I greeted her and put my palm in hers. Afterward, I was like, "Oh my gosh, Shawn just touched me! I'm training with an Olympic athlete!" It was pretty thrilling. Over the following months, we trained side by side and shared so many good, hard laughs—and when Chow and Li weren't training me, Shawn offered me additional coaching and advice on the sidelines. I already admired her from afar—but up close, I respected her even more, mostly because she goes after what she wants. She has a "catch me if you can" attitude that makes her mentally strong.

Not long after I began training with Chow, I knew I'd made the right choice. For starters, my body transformed practically overnight. I left Virginia Beach weighing eighty-four pounds with moderate tone. Under Chow's guidance, I quickly put on ten pounds of pure muscle mass and developed the most well-defined guns I've ever had.

I also had an up-close experience of the warmth I'd felt between Chow and Shawn Johnson at the Beijing Olympics. What makes Chow so amazing isn't just his competence as a coach; it's his care for and belief in his students. "If you have the talent and you work hard enough," he often told me and my teammates, "you can achieve anything." His own journey from Beijing to Des Moines is certainly proof of that.

Saying good-bye to John and Joyelle was pretty tough—but hugging Mom and Arielle for the last time before they flew back to Virginia was even harder. "I love you, baby girl," Mom told me, cupping my face in her palms.

"Remember, you can Skype me anytime. I'm always just one call away, and God is with you all the time."

I stayed temporarily with one host family and eventually moved to my more permanent home away from home — with Travis and Missy Parton and their four daughters. Mom settled me into the first family's home then returned a few months later to visit me at the Partons' house. By the time I moved into the Partons' place, Mom, Travis, and Missy had already talked at length — about everything from their parenting approach to the faith Mom had raised me with. I was relieved and happy when Mom told me the Partons were Christians who attended church — at least we already had something in common. I didn't actually meet the Partons in person until my short time with that initial family had ended.

I was busy doing my homework at Chow's gym when Missy first approached me — one of her daughters, Leah, trains at Chow's place, so Missy had arrived to pick her up. Mom and Missy had also arranged for Missy to connect with me on this particular day.

"Hello, Gabrielle, I'm Missy," she said, flashing a broad smile. "I'm the one who's going to be hosting you." As I greeted her in return, a single thought reeled through my brain: *Oh my goodness, this woman looks so much like Katherine Heigl!* Everything from Missy's long blonde tresses to the way she laughed reminded me of the actress.

A few moments later, I met her daughter, then just six. She had golden hair and bluish-green eyes. "This is

Leah," Missy introduced. "Hey, Leah," I said, smiling—but Leah didn't say a word. "Why are you being so shy?" Missy said with a chuckle.

Missy drove us to her house, which seemed like such a long distance back then, mostly because I didn't know exactly where we would end up. The whole time, as we drove onto gravel roads and then kept going … and going … and going, I was thinking, *Where in the world does this family live?* The whole way there, Missy and I exchanged small talk.

"What do you like to eat?" Missy asked.

I listed a bunch of items, like fruit.

"Do you love strawberries?" she asked.

"Yes," I said, "especially chocolate-covered ones!" We laughed. I was already getting along so well with Missy that I actually thought, *Aw man, why can't Missy be a single parent? What if her husband doesn't like me?*

We finally pulled into the driveway of a purplish, two-story house with a big, grassy front yard. Inside, things were a bit wild at first: the Partons' daughters were running all over the place! In addition to six-year-old Leah and her twin sister, Lexi, there was the oldest daughter, Hailey, then eight; and the youngest, Elissa, then three. Travis was in the kitchen preparing dinner: grilled chicken with mashed potatoes and fruit. When he heard us come through the front door, he met us there.

"Hi, Gabby, I'm Travis!" he said cheerfully and with a bit of a laugh.

"I'm Gabrielle," I said, suddenly feeling almost as shy

has Leah had seemed. Travis called in the other girls, who also turned bashful when they saw me—but trust me, that timidity didn't take long to wear off!

We all sat down around a long table that Travis crafted (he builds beautiful furniture!), held hands, and prayed. "Lord, thank you for bringing Gabrielle into our home," Travis said. I peeked through one eye to have a closer look at everyone's faces around the table; I quickly closed that eye again when I saw that the other four girls were peeking too. "And God, please bless our food," Travis continued. "In your name we pray, amen."

After we'd devoured the chicken (delish!), Travis placed dessert on the table: a bowl of fresh strawberries, grapes, and apples. Once the fruit was on my plate, I picked up a strawberry and casually popped it into my mouth.

"Ooh, that's gross!" one of the girls said. "You're eating with your hands!"

I froze. Travis could tell I was embarrassed, and I think he and Missy were too. So he broke the tension by saying, "Girls, come on! We eat strawberries with our hands all the time." I'd later discover that was completely true—but on that first night, I thought, *If I have to be super polite around this family, this is going to be very awkward.*

Before bedtime, Travis turned to me and said, "Welcome to our home, Gabby. Let us know if you need anything at all. What's ours is yours." I was starting to see that Travis and I would get along just fine. The girls all hugged me before Missy showed me the rooms where I could sleep.

Compared to our small town house back in Virginia Beach, this house seemed huge. On the main level, where I'd entered that evening, there was the living room, a dining room, and a kitchen; the family's four bedrooms were upstairs. And then there was the basement. "You can have the whole basement to yourself," Missy told me, "or we can give you a bedroom upstairs." At first, having a space of my own seemed heavenly, but after a couple nights down there, I felt too lonely; I wasn't used to having my own room or even my own bed! So one morning over breakfast, I asked Missy, "Can I move upstairs with the rest of the family?" The answer was yes. So the twins shared a room; Missy and Travis had the master bedroom; and Hailey and Elissa shared a room right across from mine.

In my new room upstairs, the queen bed was on the left of the doorway; the bed was neatly dressed with a set of crisp, cotton sheets. Once I pulled back the covers and climbed in wearing my PJs, I just lay there for several minutes staring straight up at the ceiling. I wondered what TV show John and Joy were watching that night. I thought about what it would feel like to curl up with Zoway. I remembered the words Mom had left me with at the airport—her reassurance that no matter where I was, God was right there with me. I then turned off the light, pulled my whale, Willy, up close to my neck, and fell right to sleep.

The Letter

My father came home from Afghanistan in October 2011. Joy and John gathered at the military base with Dad's parents to greet him and welcome him home. When my father and his family hadn't asked about me by the time he and my siblings were preparing to leave, Joy finally said to everyone, "Brie's doing good in Iowa, just in case you want to know."

Dad hadn't called or met the Partons, and he hadn't shown much interest in my whereabouts. But I guess Joy's comment put me back on his mind, because not long after, a letter arrived in the mail. It was from my father—and it was incorrectly addressed to "Randy and Misty Parton." In the letter, Dad offered appreciation to the Partons for hosting me. What he didn't offer was a cent of support. I'm not saying that my father never sent money to our family. My mother says that he did at times, and that has been acknowledged in these pages. What I am saying is this: when Dad did come through, it was often with far less than enough.

Each time I looked down at the mistaken names on the front of that envelope, I was filled with embarrassment and sadness. My greatest heartbreak wasn't realizing Dad didn't know the two people who'd taken me in. It was wondering whether he cared. That's a question I live with even now.

Chapter Fifteen

*Cast all your anxiety on him because
he cares for you.*
—I PETER 5:7, NIV

AS PLAYFUL, FRIENDLY, AND WARM AS CHOW IS, MAKE NO MISTAKE—
he and his wife, Li, have the highest expectations and
standards for every one of their gymnasts. So as I prepared
for my first big meet under Chow's guidance—the Visa
National Championships in August 2011—the intensity
of our training increased. I'd promised him my full effort,
and in return, he was giving me his. In just a few months,
he increased the difficulty level of my routines by a full
four points. I was ready.

Or so I thought.

Ten weeks before my make-it-or-break-it Nationals, I
heard a pop in my leg while I was doing a leap in a floor
exercise. The upcoming competition was one of the most
critical of my career: doing well at Nationals could mean
earning the chance to compete at Worlds—and if you

don't make it to Worlds, you usually don't make it onto the Olympic team. So the timing for this injury couldn't have been worse. My entire dream was on the line.

Missy rushed me to an orthopedic surgeon, who confirmed our biggest fear: I had sprained my hamstring and injured my hip flexor. I Skyped Mom immediately.

"What am I going to do?" I said, fighting back tears.

"You're going to do what you've always done—trust God to carry you through it," she answered. "You've got to keep fighting, Brie." She'd be there in person to be sure that I did: Mom had already booked a flight to come watch me perform in St. Paul, Minnesota. I hadn't seen her since December 2010, when she, Joy, and John (Arie couldn't get off work!) came all the way to throw a pool party for my birthday and spend the holidays with me.

In the following weeks, Missy took me back to the surgeon so I could receive a cortisone injection—a remedy for pain and inflammation. The orthopedic surgeon was uncomfortable doing the procedure on me because I was so small—so the area where the shot was to be administered was even smaller than normal. He referred us to an anesthesiologist, who specialized in working on small children. The procedure was done in the hospital because the needle had to be guided into the small area with special equipment.

On the day of the shot, I grabbed Willy on my way out the door and headed to the hospital. Once there, I asked the doctor, "Is this going to hurt?" Before he could answer, he'd already sunk the longest needle I've ever seen into my behind so he could get it into an area called my hip bursa. He then pushed the needle all the way down into the bone. Ow! I pulled Willy close and squeezed his body tightly as I squelched an audible yelp.

In spite of my injury, Chow did everything he could to prepare me for the meet. Even as I worked through the pain, he wanted me to be safe so I wouldn't risk reinjury. But do you think that slowed me down? I went to physical therapy twice a day and scheduled plenty of follow-up visits to the surgeon. I wanted this victory—and badly. It would take more than a hip flexor—and hamstring— injury to stop me.

Yet as the championship got closer, that spirit of resilience wavered and my mood spiraled downward. "Why am I going through this?" I asked God one evening just as I was getting into bed. In the space of a response, there was deafening silence. Until one Sunday morning when I went to church with the Partons. That's when I heard a sermon that seemed directed at me. " 'For I know the plans I have for you,' declares the LORD," the pastor read from Jeremiah 29:11, the Scripture on which that morning's message was based. " 'Plans to prosper you and not to harm you, plans to give you hope and a future.' " In other words, God already knew how this would turn out—and that thought really touched me. As Mom had reminded me so many times, I just had to trust Him.

On the morning of the meet, I nonetheless awakened with a funny feeling in the pit of my stomach. My mind was clouded with self-doubt. *Will I be able to perform my skills, even after an injury?* Yes, I was physically prepared—but mentally, I wasn't confident at all. The sprain and weeks of recovery had thrown me off. I tried to summon that same strength David once used to battle Goliath, but weakness is all I felt.

Day one at the Visa Championship was a colossal disaster. During a single ninety-second balance beam routine, I fell completely off the beam not once, not twice, but three times! I performed so poorly that I didn't even want to compete on the second day. "Why wasn't God there for me?" I cried to Mom. "I prayed, I quoted Scripture—I did it all. I feel like He abandoned me."

Mom didn't miss a beat before offering me another perspective. "We don't always understand the big picture of why God allows us to have certain experiences," she explained. "You just have to put today behind you and focus on what you'll do tomorrow. You can do this. It's time to persevere."

Day two was better—but not by much. A couple of my routines were riddled with mistakes. In the end, the best I could pull off was a bronze medal on the uneven bars and seventh place in the all-around. Not bad—but certainly less than I'd been expecting of myself. Now do you understand why I still call this one of the toughest competitions of my gymnastics career? Not only did I feel like I failed myself, I felt like I failed Chow—a coach who, despite his initial reservations, had taken me on.

When my mother first talked to Chow about moving me to West Des Moines, she told him there was no way our family could move there with me. "I'll check to see if there's a family willing to take her in," he'd told Mom. At that point, the Partons weren't even in the picture yet. Let me explain why that became so important at this point in my life.

When Mom and I boarded our flight from Virginia Beach to West Des Moines, neither of us had any idea about who my host family would turn out to be. Talk about a leap of faith! It was only after I'd already been in Iowa for a few days that we arranged for me to stay with a temporary host family. Then while I was living there, Chow received a surprising email. It was from Missy Parton. Here is a portion of that note:

Chow,

Travis wanted me to email you and tell you that we have been feeling God's calling us to help a gymnast that may be looking and qualified to train with you from another state. Through our friendship with another family, we know that sometimes a gymnast wants to train out of state, but the family can't move. I don't know that this happens with you, but I assume that with the level of training you provide, and the world-class facility you have, that it may have or will in the future.

All we are asking is that you keep us in mind if there is a gymnast who wants to train and will be an excellent addition to your team, but whose family does not have the means to get her here otherwise. We have a home with space to provide a room. We have four girls that would love another "sister." And we live very nearby.

I hope that you see our heart and our desire to be good stewards with what God has blessed us with. We want to provide an opportunity to someone who may not otherwise get it. If you have any questions or want to discuss this more, just let us know. Thanks for listening.

Missy (and Travis) Parton

Months before Missy emailed that note to Chow, she and her family had lived through a very difficult time: Missy lost her mother to ovarian cancer following a three-and-a-half-year battle. "She was one of my best friends," Missy later told me of her mother. "She was very involved in my kids' lives as well. After we lost her, we were just trying to figure out what life would look like without Mom." She also remembered a comment that Missy's father once made: "God loves us too much to let us keep living with the void created after losing your mom. He will find something to fill it with—not necessarily replace it, but fill it."

Around that time, Travis got an idea. One morning as he was praying, he says he felt God leading him to take in an Olympic hopeful at Chow's gym. At first, he thought it was a crazy idea. But when the thought wouldn't go away, he finally mentioned it to Missy. They agreed that they should indeed open up their home. Not that they needed anything extra to do.

For about five years, they've owned a home-maintenance business. Together, they run the business from their house and raise their four young daughters. Yet Travis just couldn't shake the feeling that he should contact Chow.

Chow thanked the Partons for their offer, and a few months later, he called to take them up on it. "There's a gymnast here who needs a host," he explained. Enter me—an Olympic dreamer who'd appeared from a world away. Once my time with the first family ended, Mom flew back to Des Moines to meet the Partons in person and settle me in with the family. Their home and family turned out to be perfect for me.

By the time I moved in with Missy and Travis, I'd noticed something around town—I could go days without seeing another black person. It was weird! When Mom came to town, she and I started to joke about it. We turned it into slug bug—an old game people play when they're on road trips. Here's how the game goes: whenever someone spots a Volkswagen Beetle (often called a Bug), he or she yells out, "Slug bug!" and then playfully arm-punches the other passengers. Well, Mom and I came up with our own version (though we called our game by another name, "punch buggy"), and I continued that with Travis and Missy. Each time we saw someone black, we'd arm-punch each other and say, "Black person!" Other times, if we noticed an African American at church, for instance, Missy would chuckle while saying, "Hey, you got a sister over there!" I found that hilarious. Still do.

In September 2011, after the catastrophe at the Visa National Championship, I flew to the Károlyi ranch in Texas for something called a World Championship verification camp. You see, just because you're on the national team doesn't mean you automatically get to represent Team USA and compete at upcoming meets. As national team members, we have to complete our routines well and earn our spots to compete at international meets. I knew this was my chance to redeem myself by working harder than ever and demonstrating my skills on the apparatuses. That's exactly what I did—and Márta Károlyi chose me for a spot on the 2011 World Championship team. Hallelujah.

Many people were surprised and even a little miffed that I was selected to be a part of the 2011 World Championship team. In a way, being in the underdog position gave me fuel: I worked hard to prove myself. Among sports commentators and in gymnastics circles, many said that I couldn't handle the pressure of elite competition on the national and international stages and that I had trouble focusing. Yes, I'd fallen off the beam—but I was also performing with a major injury. Yet Mom and my coach never allowed me to use excuses; they instead urged me to get to work. To this day when others doubt me, their uncertainty drives me to double my efforts.

So I pushed harder in physical therapy even as Chow

and Li trained me like never before. "Forget what other people are saying," Chow told me. "I believe you're mentally tough. You're strong. You're focused. And I know you can do this." We all knew what was at stake: my chances of ever making it to London were largely contingent upon a single competition—the 2011 World Championships in Tokyo, Japan.

Chapter Sixteen

Discouragement and failure are two of the surest stepping stones to success.

—Dale Carnegie

As the baby in my own family, I felt weird suddenly becoming the oldest girl in the Parton house. After I'd settled into the family and gotten to know Travis, he and I were chatting one evening. "You know, you could really be a role model for these other girls," he told me. *Huh?* I thought. *I don't think so, Travis. I've never been anyone's role model. I'm the youngest of my siblings, remember?* But the more time I spent time with the adorable Parton girls, the more clearly I could see Travis's point.

Leah, one of the twins, had already been training at Chow's gym by the time I arrived; all the Parton girls started dance classes when they were three, but Missy had noticed that Leah's personality didn't fit dancing. She was always climbing up on Travis's shoulders and seemed to have great balance. "Why don't you take her to the gym?" a friend suggested. Leah had loved it immediately.

"Wanna go on the trampoline with me?" Leah would ask. The two of us would jump forever out in the backyard, just as I had done with Beka, John, and Joyelle at home in Virginia Beach. I would sometimes show Leah new skills or help her refine the ones she'd learned at the gym. When we weren't bounding up and down, we were laying next to each other on the trampoline and just chatting.

"Do you ever want to go to the Olympics?" I once asked her.

"Yes, I'd like to try," she told me.

"If you keep training and working hard," I told her, "anything is possible. And one more thing: If you ever get scared of a big skill, just come talk to me. I've been there." She looked over at me and smiled, then we both got up and kept flipping. I was starting to like my new role as a role model!

During the school year, my gym time ran from two thirty to six thirty. So my morning schedule at the Parton place went something like this: Breakfast at nine in the morning (usually cereal), right around the time Missy was back from driving the girls to school; by nine thirty, I was starting my homeschool work up in my room. (Elissa, who was just three and a half and not yet in kindergarten when I first moved in, would curl up at the foot of my bed with her toy computer to copy me as I typed on my MacBook—so cute!) After I'd finished my homework,

Missy and I would sometimes hang out and talk, or climb into the Chevy Suburban and swing by Hy-Vee grocery store to pick up some items for dinner.

Dinnertime—that was an immovable daily appointment in the Parton house. By the time Missy picked me up from Chow's and we rounded the corner back to the house, supper was usually already in the works. Missy makes a mean ham ball—a kind of mouthwatering meatball that contains a mix of beef, pork, and, of course, ham. It's got sauce on it, and she bakes it in the oven. It was one of the first recipes she cooked up after I arrived, and I've loved it ever since the first bite. There's just one thing that can make ham balls more delicious—a side of cheesy potatoes. Divine!

"Who wants to pray?" Travis asked before supper one night, as he always did; the other girls would usually fling their hands up in the air and go, "Me! I wanna pray!" But I was usually too shy to be the one to pray. *What if I stutter?* I thought. *Or what if I say the wrong thing?* That's why everyone looked a little surprised when I volunteered for the first time. We all locked hands, closed our eyes, and lowered our heads. "Thank you, God, for this beautiful day," I whispered, hoping I wouldn't stumble over my words. "Thank you, God, for blessing everyone, and help us to accomplish what we set our minds to. Bless this food and our bodies. Amen." *Phew, I made it through that one!*

After dinner, the girls would sometimes play around or wrestle with Travis in the middle of the living room. "I got ya!" Travis would yell out, holding on to Hailey's ankle. Meanwhile, Elissa, Leah, or Lexi would be squirming to break free of the grip he had on them with his other hand. Sometimes, I'd swoop in to help them break free. "Come on, Lexi!" I'd say, dragging her up by her right arm. A family fight club—so fun!

In addition to our family times, I often chilled and chatted one-on-one with Travis or Missy. For me, Travis felt like a father and a big brother combined in one—and oh, how I missed John, my sidekick! That's why I was especially excited when Travis would utter the sentence I looked forward to every couple weeks: "Wanna grab a movie tonight?" He and I saw every type of flick you can imagine, from action to comedy. Though he's not a big fan of vampires, I once twisted his arm into taking me to the midnight showing of the third Twilight movie. Now that's a friend! And in the months to come, as my training with Chow grew more strenuous and I rounded the corner toward my goal, I'd have to lean on that friendship like never before.

After a 9.0-magnitude earthquake and a tsunami devastated the residents of Japan in March 2011, and the resulting nuclear situation filled the air with toxins, the International Federation of Gymnastics officials considered moving the World Championships to another city. They ultimately decided to keep the games in Tokyo. By October, the air quality had become safe again.

I'd never been to Japan. So when I arrived in Tokyo with the women's team, the capital was a feast for my senses: Lush green gardens dotted with colorful pagodas. Immaculate boulevards lined with couture shops. The smell of miso soup's rich broth wafting through myriad homes and high-rise apartments. And people—millions of them, it seemed—sashaying through the streets and city squares. Truly a world away from West Des Moines and Virginia Beach!

At fifteen, I was the youngest competitor on the US team. Going into Worlds, a lot of people perceived me as the team's uneven bar specialist. And with good reason: Chow had coached me in mastering the kinds of skills that lifted me high up into the air above the uneven bars. I'd used his techniques to claim the silver medal at the U.S. CoverGirl Classic in July 2011. "A great bar routine is like a beautiful song," Chow once told me. "It should have a nice rhythm and flow, and it should be as graceful as it is powerful." A bar performance is passion and lyrical poetry in the form of sport. And it's as close as I've ever come to actually soaring.

The crazy thing is that I once hated bars. "I suck at bars," I'd often tell Mom. "I'm never going to be any good at them."

"You'll continue to struggle if you speak so negatively," my mother told me. She quoted Proverbs 23:7 ("As a man thinketh in his heart, so is he") and Proverbs 18:21 ("Life and death are in the power of the tongue: and they that love it shall eat the fruit thereof") from the KJV. So I started to change the way I thought and talked about the uneven bars. "I enjoy bars and will one day be great at it," I'd say to myself instead. And over time, I began to believe that. As Chow improved my technique, my performance also improved. What you think, believe, and repeat will often come true for you.

I awakened on the morning of the competition feeling pretty jittery. Nerves just happen when you're facing a pivotal competition — and I knew this was my chance to literally show the world what I was capable of at an international meet. As I laid out my purplish-blue leo and pulled my hair into a scrunchie, I asked God for His help. I didn't get down on my knees; Mom has always told me that God hears our prayers whether we're standing, sitting, kneeling, or even half asleep. That's because it's not about the position of your body; it's about the position of your heart. As I used little clips to hold back a few disobedient strands of hair, I prayed the simplest prayer I knew: "Lord, you've promised to give me strength," I whispered. "I need that strength today. Amen."

Every gymnast on the team was counting on the girl next to her, which meant every routine needed to be superior during team qualifications. I competed in all four events. We were all feeling anxious because we lost our team captain, Alicia Sacramone, who tore her Achilles tendon while we were training beforehand. I placed third for the US, but unfortunately — because of the two-gymnasts-per-country rule — I didn't qualify for the all-around competition. I was very disappointed. When

I mounted the beam for my routine during team qualifications, I could sense everyone in the arena holding their breath, just as I had been holding mine all day. But can you believe I got through the entire ninety-second routine without a single fall? Aside from a few bobbles here and there, my other routines were solid as well. Major exhale!

That day, God answered my prayer — big time. With a combined score of 179.411, Team USA edged out Russia and China to win the gold. "We did it!" my teammates yelled practically in unison as we huddled and high-fived at the sidelines. The tears I cried that day were born not just of euphoria, but of relief. I hadn't achieved my ultimate goal — I wanted to come home as the all-around world champion — but I had proven something to myself and others. When the pressure was on, I could deliver.

I'd accomplished something else as well: I qualified for uneven bar finals. After grazing my foot on the high bar during the routine (hey, it happens!), I placed fifth. Yet the strong bar routine I performed during team finals was still a big hit with at least one person — Márta Károlyi. She noticed just how high I was flying on my release skills, and she gave me a nickname afterward: the Flying Squirrel. At first, I thought, *Really? A squirrel? Why not Supergirl or Wonder Woman — they fly, right? Then again, at least squirrels are cute, so I'll take it!* Good thing I made peace with the name. It stuck.

As our team won gold, I watched the other girls' moms hugging in celebration. I yearned to have my mother there too! Because the overseas trip was so expensive, she hadn't been able to afford the flight. I knew that, but that didn't make it hurt any less. More and more as the months snaked by, I missed her. Terribly. And in a way, experiencing the thrill of an enormous win made the disappointment of not having her there even more pronounced. "God is always right beside you," Mom would remind me. But the truth is that I felt alone. Very alone.

From the floor of the arena that night amid the jubilation, I called Mom. "I'm ... all ... by ... myself!" I sobbed into the phone. "I'm ... so ... alone!" I was so distraught that my mother could hardly decipher my words. She tried to console me, but I cried even more.

"Baby girl, calm down and take a breath," she said. "You know I'd be there if I could. I promise you this: I will never miss another meet. Ever. No matter how much it costs, I will find a way to get there." Just then, Missy beeped in on Mom's line, and my mother put her on the line. She thought hearing Missy's voice would make me feel better, but I began crying again! Once I finally caught my breath, I told Mom I'd Skype when I returned to my room. I did.

When I arrived back in Des Moines, Mom surprised me with something far more precious than a silver or gold medal: she had traveled to Iowa that day just so she could hold me once more.

The Conversations

For the twenty-two months I lived in Iowa, I talked with my father four, maybe five, times. Actually, we texted more than we talked. But after Team USA won the gold at the World Championships in Tokyo, Dad neither texted nor called. He didn't keep up with my career as a gymnast—which is why he had no idea how important the milestone was. More than anything, I wanted him to pay attention. In my heart, I'd always hoped that he actually cared. I still hope that.

"Do you want to plan a fishing trip?" Dad wrote to me in one text. "I can't wait for you to come home." The crazy thing is that for several years, I'd been awaiting that exact kind of invitation from him. A few weeks after I received Dad's text, Travis came into the kitchen one morning. "Missy," he announced, "I think I'll plan a trip to go ice fishing." My heart froze. Just hearing that sentence made me miss Dad all the more.

Chapter Seventeen

Oh, Auntie Em, there's no place like home.
— DOROTHY IN THE WIZARD OF OZ

CHRISTMAS PEEKED FROM AROUND THE CORNER. AS FALL GAVE WAY TO winter and the sycamores stretched naked toward the sky, Iowa grew chilly. The hours of sunlight diminished slowly by the day, making dusk descend far too soon. In just a few short weeks, I would celebrate a milestone. I was turning sixteen.

"Joy to the world, the Lord is come!" From the ice-filled tub where I soaked my feet every few days, I could overhear the radio tune, one that always made me think of my beloved sister. I absolutely hate soaking in ice, especially when it's already freezing outside. But when you're an elite gymnast, an ice tub is just a fact of life: the intensity of the training puts constant strain on the joints. I usually got through the soaks by blasting music in my ears—like "Superstar" and "Enchanted," or any random mix of hits I could string together on my iPod. But that night, I'd stepped into the tub without my earphones and instead imagined the holiday to come.

"Let earth receive her king," crooned the carolers on the radio. Mom, Joyelle, and John had already given me the best gift I could ever ask for; they were flying to spend Christmas in West Des Moines. They'd come for my big birthday and then ring in the New Year with me. As their visit drew closer, I caught myself daydreaming about it during my sessions at the gym. Li was training me on the beam. Chow oversaw my routines on the vault, bars, and floor. Our sessions were increasing in difficulty as the calendar marched toward the Olympic year.

I loved living with the Partons. Yet nothing could replace the comfort, the familiarity, the immeasurable pleasure of simply sitting around in my PJs with my own family. Or smelling Mom's matzo ball soup from the kitchen stove. Or curling up beside Zoway and Chan Chan. Across the months and miles, we'd all stayed in touch as best we could: Joy and I would always Skype or call each other after our weekly must-see show, *The Vampire Diaries.* I talked with Mom just about every day, and she'd usually put John and Arielle on the line. Most of our calls ended the same way. "I love you, Boo Tookie Boo!" (another of Mom's many nicknames for me). Once we hung up, my mother's final words still hanging in the air, I missed my family even more.

"And heaven, and heaven, and nature sing ..." The chorus trailed off as I reflected on the time I'd already spent away from Virginia Beach—the rigorous workouts, made far easier by the fun I shared with some of the other gymnasts. Sierra, Courtney, Vicky, Alexis, Nora, Tina—from September to January to December, day in and day out, so many of the girls at Chow's gym became sisters to me. We trained hard, but we laughed even harder. Some of my teammates had their sights set on gymnastics scholarships; others, like me, were dreaming of an Olympics bid. And as 2011 slowed to a finish with the holiday season, that 2012 goal felt so suddenly close.

Throughout 2011, Chow gave my skills a complete makeover. Back when I'd arrived at his gym, he'd asked me to forget the techniques I'd learned—not because they were necessarily wrong, but more because he could train me best if we started from scratch using his method. I "forgot" my skills simply by not performing them for weeks at a time; then once the old habits had fallen away, I began with a fresh approach. I was using too much effort to perform my giants on the uneven bars, for instance. Chow taught me how to relax while doing the exercise.

His approach worked—so well, in fact, that Mom was amazed when she saw how much stronger all my routines had become. "Your technique and new routines are just *amazing*!" she told me. As difficult as it was to be far away from my family, I had made the right choice to come to Iowa. The upgrade to my skills was proof of that.

With the Olympics less than a year away, I needed another upgrade—altogether new skills that were harder than any I'd learned before. That meant the skills were also scarier. Do you have any idea what it feels like to master a round-off double back on the beam? Or a double pike dismount? Or an Arabian double front leap combo on the floor? Let me tell you: it can all be pretty frightening, especially when you're first learning. We gymnasts live with the constant fear that we may fall flat on our faces or behinds, or that we'll injure ourselves in some irreparable way. In a sense, my gymnastics training can be boiled down to two words: courage and discipline. It takes plenty of chutzpah to remount a beam or bar after you've fallen countless times. "The journey of training every day—the hard work, the effort, the improvement, the progress—that's more important than getting the gold," Coach Chow once told me. "The victory isn't just about earning a medal—it's about winning every single day that you train." So true—but a gold medal is always nice too, lol.

At certain times—usually when I was missing Mom, home, and Virginia Beach—my passion and discipline waned. If my heart wasn't in my routine on a particular day, Chow would call Travis. That happened in November 2011. "You need to come pick her up right now," Chow told Travis over the phone. "I need you to reinforce for Gabrielle that she has a goal to get to the Olympics." Once I'd hopped into Travis's truck, we'd drive around and chat. He knew I was homesick, but he also knew I'd come too far to fizzle out. "You need to stay focused," he reminded me. "We're all here to support you. That's why you need to give Chow one hundred percent." On most days, I could do that. But on other days, when my training was especially tough, I had this overwhelming desire to just let go of everything.

Around mid-December, I had one of those days. The World Championships were behind me. The American Cup competition was ahead of me in March 2012. And as much as I enjoyed Missy's banana nut bread, I yearned to sit at my own mother's dining room table, elbow to elbow again with Arie, Joy, and John. *What would it be like to just forget this whole thing and go home?* I mused. *I bet I could just live on the prize money I won at Worlds.* My feelings even caught me by surprise: How could I consider giving up after all my family and I had fought for? Yet every time I tried to switch the channel on these thoughts, their refrains grew louder.

One afternoon when I was absolutely beside myself with homesickness, I began drafting a note to my mother on my cell phone. "Gymnastics is not my passion anymore," I wrote. I stopped and stared down at the sentence—six words that could mean a different life for me. It seemed crazy—too insane to say out loud or even think about. A shiver traveled up my spine. *My brother, John, is great at track*, I thought. *I've always loved Usain Bolt. Maybe I could swap gymnastics for running.* I returned my fingertips to the keyboard and continued writing: "I want to get famous off of running track." Or maybe not.

Two weeks after I started that text and one day before Christmas, my family arrived in West Des Moines. I could hardly wait for them to pull into the driveway at the Partons' house. When they finally did, I dashed out the front door to meet them.

"Breezy!" Mom screamed as she opened the car door. She ran toward me and scooped me up into her arms.

"What's up, Brie?" John said as we embraced.

Joy and I then hugged for the longest time, both of us suppressing tears. I could cry right now as I remember the moment. It was pure bliss to see my family. That night over dinner, our laughter reverberated from the Partons' walls.

Mom booked a room large enough for the five of us at Staybridge Suites. We didn't have a Christmas tree at the hotel, but Mom had packed our gifts into a suitcase. "Here you are," she said, handing each of us a carefully wrapped package.

In the following days, other than a trip to the mall, we didn't do anything all that special—and that's what makes my family so amazing. Even if we're simply sitting around, laughing and reminiscing, it's still fun—kinda like a comedy hour that stretches into twenty-four of them. Joy, John, and I got a snicker out of watching our mother sweat it out in the hotel's gym: she'd asked me to help her with a workout plan by becoming her personal trainer for the day, which was the second time she'd requested my help. I'm sure she now wishes she'd given that more thought before she opened her mouth, because I loved making her workouts impossible. "Keep going, Mom!" I shouted as she struggled to hoist her upper half toward the ceiling for a sit-up. "That's right, Mom," I said with a chuckle, "This is what I go through every day!"

To ring in my sixteenth birthday, Mom rented a room in the Raccoon River Park Nature Lodge and threw a joint party with one of my teammates, named Olivia, a gymnast who'd come over from England just to train with Chow. Mom decorated the room with pretty Sweet Sixteen decorations. Later, the guests were given big multicolored Chinese lanterns to light before they floated up into the sky. It was super cool!

Even while my family was in town, I had to drag myself to the gym in the afternoons. On the day after Christmas. And then the next day. And then the next. When you're training for the Olympics, you can't just skip out on your sessions. And I won't lie—I was starting to really hate it. It was so hard to leave Mom, Joy, and John at the hotel, especially as the end of their visit grew closer. It's not that I'd suddenly lost my passion for gymnastics; it's just that my fervor had been eclipsed by an even stronger force—an absolute ache to live under the same roof with Mom and my siblings again. The same thoughts I'd been having all month returned, this time roaring even louder: *I should end it all today and fly back to Virginia Beach with Mom, Joy, and John.*

On the morning of January 2—the day before my family would return to my hometown—I pulled out my cell phone and finished drafting that note. *If I'm going to quit,* I thought, *this is my last chance.* That afternoon, as my mother and I pulled into the driveway of Chow's gym, I reached over and handed Mom my cell phone with my note on the screen. You already know how that drama turned out. What you don't yet know is what happened between my announcement and the Olympics.

Chapter Eighteen

Flowers grow out of dark moments.
—CORITA KENT

AFTER I SHOCKED EVERYONE WITH THE ANNOUNCEMENT THAT I PLANNED
to quit, Travis tried to talk me out of it. Chow tried to
talk me out of it. And God *knows* Mom tried to talk me
out of it. But I've never told the world about the critical
conversation that actually turned things around. It was
one I had with my brother, John.

Once Mom sped out of the parking lot of Chow's gym,
we returned to Staybridge Suites. Inside the hotel, the situation got even uglier. When Mom and I walked through
the door, John was sitting on the bed eating a bowl of
Berry Cap'n Crunch cereal and watching his favorite
zombie show on the Syfy channel.

"What are you doing back here?" John asked, glancing

over at the clock to realize that it was too early for me to be done with training. I stared at John but said nothing.

"Tell John what you just told me," Mom said sharply. Joy, who was sitting on the other bed, sat up because she sensed a firestorm was coming.

"I want to quit," I said.

John lowered his spoon and set his bowl aside. "Why would you quit now?"

"Because I just don't want to do it anymore."

"That's not true!" John shouted. "You can't give up your gift, Brie!"

Just then, Joy piped up. "I can't even look at you right now," she said with the biggest sneer I've ever seen on her face. I immediately knew she was serious—Joy has rarely ever spoken a harsh word to me. "Mom's done so much for you," she continued, "and I even gave up my ice skating lessons in eighth grade because Mom couldn't afford to keep us both in a sport! Can you give me one good reason why you want to come home?!"

"I just miss you guys, and—"

"Brie, there is nothing at home for you!" Joy cut in. "Do you think you can go to school or get a job and just become a normal teenager again? You can't!" Joy then got right up in my face.

"Get back!" I shouted as I began to cry.

John wedged himself between Joy and me, trying to keep our verbal war from becoming a physical one. Mom, who'd been standing aside watching this whole WWE moment, interrupted with a commercial break. "You know what, Brie?" she said. "Get your things together. I'm taking you back to Missy and Travis's place."

That must have been the longest car ride of my life—dead silence the whole way. "If you're going to quit," Mom finally said as we got closer to the house, "you're going to be the bearer of bad news. That's right, you heard me, sister. You're going to face Márta Károlyi yourself." (Earlier, I'd asked Mom if she would make the call for me and tell Márta I was going to quit.)

Once we arrived at the Partons' home, Travis tried to give me a pep talk. It didn't work. Meanwhile, Mom and Missy drove back to the gym and met with Chow. "She's just afraid of success, of being on top," Chow concluded after he heard that I wanted to end my career. And to this day, he still thinks that's true. But honest to God, I wasn't afraid to win. I truly was just homesick. "All I can hope and pray is that she catches her vision again," Mom told Chow. "But for now, I'm leaving her here. We're going home."

The following afternoon, Mom, Joy, and John all said good-bye to me. (Shakespeare once called parting "such sweet sorrow," and I suddenly knew what the guy meant, especially when it came to the sorrow part.) By the time I arrived at the gym that afternoon, Chow had had time to consider my perspective. He told me a story of how much he'd missed his family when he'd come to Iowa from China. "I understand your homesickness," he said. "You're human. But you have to keep pushing through it, because it's all going to pay off. Just trust me. I know you can do this." Li later added her own footnote to Chow's powerful plea. "We don't sleep sometimes because we're up developing a plan for you," she said. "If we didn't believe in you, we wouldn't work so hard on your behalf."

So for the following two days, I did my duty: I dragged myself out of bed and let Missy drive me to the gym. But by the third day, it was pretty clear to Chow that my efforts were still half-hearted. He called Travis again and asked him to pick me up.

That afternoon, Travis drove me over to Raccoon River Park near the gym. "Tell me what's on your mind," he said. I repeated my Chick-fil-A idea. "Why are you going to give up on your dream to go make $7 an hour?" he said. "Don't sell yourself short." We then made a list of all the things I missed about Virginia versus the things I'd regret about leaving Iowa. "I'm going to keep this list so we can laugh about it one day," he said. I wanted to keep the whole conversation going for as long as possible so I wouldn't have to go back in the gym—so I extended it with a question. "Why can't I just go to the World Championship and finish off there?"

"Because everyone watches the Olympics, not the World Championships," he blurted out. I could always count on Travis to keep it real. "Do you want to be the gymnast who never was?"

Even after all these motivational speeches and family confrontations, I still wanted to hang up my leotards. And I was so mad at my mother that I hadn't called her. I know it sounds crazy, but my homesickness had just overtaken my brain. As far as I was concerned, the only thing I still needed to figure out was how to buy my plane ticket home. Then one night about two weeks after the biggest meltdown of my life, John called me from Virginia Beach.

"How is it that other gymnasts win a lot of big competitions, and you've got so few notches on your belt?" he asked. *Thanks a lot*, I thought. "It's unacceptable, Brie. You've got to make a living in your sport."

I fired back. "How many notches do you have on *your* belt, John?"

My brother paused. "Well at least I don't mess around in the gym," he finally said. "My coach takes me to hell and back every day, and I love every minute of it."

We both went silent on the line for a moment before John continued. "Today should always be better than yesterday," he said. "You've got to put your body on the line. Remember our motto: If you want to be the best, you've got to take out the best."

That conversation was my turning point — the wake-up call that pulled me back from my foolish reckoning. John has always been my best friend. On that evening, he also became one of the heroes of my Olympic journey.

The very next day, I started reading my Bible. Every time I got scared of one of my skills, I meditated on the verses that had anchored me through so many difficult experiences: "For God has not given us a spirit of fear, but of power and of love and of a sound mind" (2 Timothy 1:7, NKJV) and "I can do all things through Christ who strengthens me" (Philippians 4:13, NKJV). Each time I repeated the words, I could literally feel them bolstering my faith.

On January 17, 2012, I began setting weekly goals—like aiming to master five new routines within a certain number of days. I also started visualizing my victory. Mom, who has taught me to use vision boards to keep my dreams right before my eyes, gave me Habakkuk 2:2 from the KJV: "Write the vision, and make it plain upon tables, that he may run that readeth it." And on my calendar, I started marking off the days—195 more sunrises until the London Olympic games.

Chapter Nineteen

I'm always making a comeback but nobody
ever tells me where I've been.
—Billie Holiday

I CALLED IT THE FIRST REAL TEST AFTER MY TURNAROUND — THE
March 2012, AT&T American Cup. In the end, the
press called it something else. You'll see what I mean in
a second.

First things first: I wasn't originally slated to be at this
competition, which was held at New York's Madison
Square Garden. Gymnasts Jordyn Weiber and Aly
Raisman had already been chosen to represent the United
States at the meet. But after the World Championships
in Tokyo, Chow thought I needed more exposure on
an international stage. "I think there's a way to get her
in there," he told Mom. So my coach called up Márta
Károlyi and said, "I want to see if Gabrielle can compete
as an alternate." If Jordyn or Aly were injured, he
reasoned, I could step right in. That made sense to Márta.

Even when you're an alternate, you get to compete in exhibition routines. Plus, the very same judges who score the official competitors also evaluate you—only your scores don't actually count. All that was fine by Chow. He just wanted me to debut my brand-new bar routine so he could see how it would be scored before my next big meet. That's a typical move by a savvy coach.

"Remember what you told me after Worlds," my mother commented in the days leading up to the American Cup. "You said you wanted to be world champion. Well, here's an opportunity to work toward that. Plus, London is just a few months off. You need to treat every competition like it's the Olympic games. You need to go out there like, 'This is my medal, and nobody's gonna take it from me.' If you want it, you need to fight for it. I don't want to hear about what you're *trying* to do. Let me see what you're *going* to do." That was my cue to set off fireworks.

Mom, Arie, Joy, John, and Miss Carolyn all drove up to Manhattan for the big meet—and I was brimming with excitement about seeing them. From my first vault to my final tumble on the floor, I thought of every encouraging word Mom had given me—and I channeled that inspiration into my routines. Apparently, it worked: Someone tabulated my totals and realized I was leading the official competitors by nearly a point! I had nailed an Amanar vault, and it was the first time I'd ever performed it in a competition. Uneven bars were next, and that performance put me in the lead and caught the media's attention. By the time I got to beam, cameramen were knocking each other to film my routine. Of course, everyone knew my scores didn't count, but it was still stunning that I'd outperformed everyone. Can I be frank with you? As confident as I felt before that meet, even I was shocked. I'm sure the field of official contenders were too.

Though I made a big impression on those gathered, I did make my mistakes: I stepped out of bounds on my floor routine. Twice. But despite those errors and corresponding point deductions, I still ended up with a surprising result: I garnered a total score of 61.299 — nearly two-tenths ahead of the top score. In gymnastics circles, it is often said that the gymnast who wins the American Cup will go on to become the Olympic all-around champion. *Could that be true this year?* I thought. Be still, my heart!

Jordyn Weiber was declared the American Cup champion for the third time in her career, and rightfully so — both she and Aly, the dazzling silver medalist, rocked the house by delivering stellar routines. All good news for Team USA. Many also saw the 2012 American Cup as my coming-out party. And truthfully, so did I.

In the following weeks and months, the media stopped labeling me as the gymnast who buckled under pressure, the one who fumbled on the balance beam at the Visa Championships. Instead, they described me in a way that still gives me goose bumps. For the first time, I became the girl who just might grab a spot on the 2012 Olympic team.

During my time in Iowa, the Partons' house became my playhouse. Hailey and I loved running away from Lexi, Leah, and Elissa, simply because they loved the fun of chasing us. "Come back here!" they'd yell. We'd of course dart in the other direction.

One day when Hailey and I were running too fast from the youngest three girls, I slipped on a mat and fell to my knees. "Are you all right?" Hailey asked, laughing a bit. I was fine—but oh, my knees ached! I was practically limping when I got up, but not so much so that it stopped me from scheming. "Okay, Hailey, let's go hide from the others," I whispered. We then tiptoed our way into the twins' bedroom and slid behind the double doors of their closet. "Where could they be?" we could hear the girls asking each other. A few minutes later, the closet doors creaked open.

"I found you guys!" Elissa shouted.

"Let's run, Gabby!" Hailey said. But as she sprung from the closet, the door stopped right in front of her forehead and—*bam*!—she knocked herself out flat onto the ground. Literally.

Okay, relax: Hailey wasn't seriously injured. She stayed down on the floor a couple moments, seeing lots of stars, but then she finally opened her eyes and stumbled back up to her feet. "Oh my gosh, that was awesome!" Later as I repeated the story to Missy and Travis, we all cracked up—especially Hailey, who now always thinks twice before a game of run-and-hide.

Sometimes we took our horseplay outdoors. And speaking of horses, I actually saw one in real life. We rode our bikes down the street to meet Thunder, a stallion owned by the Partons' neighbors. I'm sure you've guessed that I—someone who'd once daydreamed about horses during countless *Wildfire* episodes—flipped out when I spotted Thunder. Well, I did. Missy sent us off with cut-up apples and carrots so we could feed the horse as we pet him.

When the temperature dipped below freezing in Iowa (I'm talking 13 degrees and colder, people!), that curtailed our time outdoors. But it didn't completely keep us inside. Just as I had on a few occasions in Virginia, I tromped out to play in the snow. The girls and I could hardly even walk because we were wearing so many layers! Two pairs of pants, five pairs of socks, a shirt, a jacket, a heavy coat, gloves, hats, and earmuffs—you name it. We had to keep the frostbite away.

Once outside, we'd all wrestle in the snow, start snowball fights, lay down to create angels, and build the tallest snowmen. As you can probably tell, there wasn't just a light dusting of flakes—sometimes, we'd get three feet or more. "Are you planning to close the gym?" I'd ask Chow in a tone that told him my question was really a cry for help in disguise. "No," he'd answer without cracking a smile. Let me tell you something about Chow: that man never closed down that gym. He and Li were hard core!

When I showed up at the gym during winter months, I sported all the same layers: my coaches were intent on keeping me healthy, especially before a competition. Even once winter melted into spring, Li gave me recommendations for how to dress. "Don't start wearing shorts just because you see the other girls wearing them," she said. "Wear pants to stay warm."

Whatever the season, I enjoyed being stylish, and I loved experimenting with my hair. Though I had to wear it up and out of the way during training, I usually let it fall loosely over my shoulders on the weekends. I also usually painted my nails to match my leo—whether purple, blue, orange, neon green. I'd sometimes give my nails some splash by adding a flower or heart design.

My growing love for fashion extended to the competition floor. For some meets, like the Visa Championships and U.S. Classics, I got to design my own leo. GK, the gymnastics sportswear company, sent me fabric swatches beforehand. Mom, Missy, and my sisters then helped me create my custom leos. "How does this look next to my skin?" I'd ask, holding the little square cloth close to my hand.

"I like that one, but let's look at the others as well," Mom would say. The choices were seemingly endless: velvet, shiny, matte, colorful. Once I'd chosen a swatch, I tried to bling it out. Love the sparkles!

After my breakout moment during the American Cup, I became especially excited about the forthcoming string of competitions. I had the Pacific Rim Championships later that same month followed by the U.S. Classics in May. Next came the Visa Championships in June. And then finally—*finally!*—the Olympic trials in July. Oh, baby.

Chapter Twenty

For everyone born of God overcomes the world.
This is the victory that has overcome the world,
even our faith.

—1 JOHN 5:4, NIV

SOME PEOPLE NEED THE PROSPECT OF MONEY TO GET MOTIVATED. FOR
me, all it takes is a puppy. So just before the Visa
Championships in 2012, Travis gave me a challenge. "If
you win gold," he told me, "you and the girls can get a
dog." Deal.

Our bet actually began back in 2011 as a bit of a joke.
I missed Zoway and Chan Chan so much that I started
lobbying the Partons for a dog. Their daughters had been
wanting a pet too, and since Travis and Missy are allergic
to cats, a puppy seemed like the perfect pick. "I don't need
another thing to take care of," Missy protested. "I already
have five girls." So by conjuring up my very best puppy-
dog eyes, I got Travis on my side. "Bring me home a gold

for the individual all-around," he teased, "and then we'll bring home a doggie." I indeed came back from Tokyo with a gold—just not the exact one we'd agreed on.

So from then on out, every time I had a big competition coming up, Trevor re-extended his offer. I came close with my upset at the American Cup—but as an alternate, I couldn't actually win a medal. A couple weeks later at Pacific Rim Championships in Everett, Washington, I had a rough meet. Because of that hip flexor and hamstring injury months before, Chow scaled back a lot on my vault training and lowered my routine's difficulty level; he wanted to give my body enough time to recover long before the Olympics. I was still working on performing my two-and-a-half vault consistently. I'd nailed it at the American Cup a couple of weeks earlier, but in Everett I wasn't as successful. My hand slipped off of the vault table. I tried to twist my body in the air to make it around two and a half times, but I landed short and badly sprained my ankle. Later in the meet, those same injuries led to my fall on the balance beam, which stirred up more talk that I cracked under pressure. But I made a comeback by scoring gold on the uneven bars, and our team went golden as well—but those two still weren't the types I needed to get a puppy. Sigh.

Next up was U.S. Secret Classics in Chicago, Illinois, on May 26, 2012. I didn't perform my vault because Chow and Li thought it was best to play it safe with the Olympics so close and my ankle injury somewhat fresh. I needed more time to work on perfecting that vault in the gym before performing it in competition again. That's why I only competed in three events: uneven bars, balance beam, and floor exercise. And I knew what that meant—there'd be no all-around medal at this competition since I wouldn't get a score for vault.

By the time the 2012 Visa Championships in St. Louis, Missouri, rolled around, I'd fixed my gaze on two goals: 1) performing well enough to be chosen for the women's national team (which meant I could compete in the Olympic trials ... yippee!), and 2) finally earning that pooch for me and the Parton girls.

Well, one out of two isn't bad, right? At Visa, I got a full point deduction after I fell off the balance beam. Bummer. And yet even after such a big mistake, my overall score was only two tenths less than the top score, which means I seized the silver. I'll take the number two spot in the country and a place on the women's national team—even if that doesn't come with a pet doggie on the side! Plus, I still had a shot. "If you win all-around at the Olympic trials," Travis said with a laugh, "my offer stands." With those words, I was off to San Jose, California, for the biggest competition of my career.

When I showed up in San Jose in June 2012, I knew I'd arrived at the moment I'd been working toward since I was eight. My dream came down to this one meet.

The competition was spread out over two days, and I got off to a strong start on the first night. My score was only three-tenths behind the top one. That evening,

I'd looked out into the audience to see my father in the stands. Though he'd mentioned that he may come, actually spotting him there surprised me; I hadn't seen him in two years. "Dad's here," I told Mom after the first evening, "and he's talking to the media."

"Don't worry about that," she told me. "Brie, I need you to focus on your performance. You have an opportunity to win this thing. You're only a few tenths behind the top score."

The following night, Mom's words reeled through my head. I thought of all the hard work, the difficult times, the move from Iowa to Virginia, the countless sacrifices my family had made for me to have this amazing opportunity. I also held on tightly to one of the many verses I've used to get me through the most difficult moments: "He shall give His angels charge over thee, to keep thee" (Luke 4:10, KJV). I said these words over and over under my breath.

On the second night of trials, I went out there and delivered the finest performance that I could muster. As I mounted the apparatuses, I could literally sense God's presence and power. He had indeed sent His angels to keep me safe as I soared high in the air during my routines. After my last tumbling pass, I whispered a simple prayer: "Thank you, God." If that's the last prayer I ever say in my life, it is enough.

The scoreboard inside the HP Pavilion told the story—my cumulative score of 123.450 put me in the top spot. It was official: my Olympic trials were not only great, but they were also golden! Not only did I win the entire competition — by doing so, I also earned the only guaranteed spot on the Olympic Team! That's right: I would proudly wear my red, white, and blue as part of Team USA in 2012. It still feels surreal.

And of course, I finally delivered the exact gold medal I needed to complete my challenge. The Partons haven't yet picked out that puppy for the girls, but you'd better believe I'll make sure they remember their promise forever. That's right, Travis — we're all still listening for that bark!

The Trials

"I have a surprise for you," my father texted me shortly before my trip to the Olympic trials in San Jose. "I'm coming to trials." Though we hadn't talked much when Dad was in Afghanistan, I wanted my father to come. During one of our few conversations by phone, I told him that. Yet I wasn't sure whether he'd actually show up.

At trials, I was warming up at the bar when I heard someone calling me: "Gabby! Gabby!" I recognized that voice, and when I turned around, it was my dad. But since he usually calls me Brie or Scooter, I was baffled by why he was screaming that name. Afterward, when the media asked me about our reunion, I said I was happy to see him again. That was only half of the truth. The other half is that I felt the same way I feel whenever Dad just turns up — equally excited and perplexed.

After the competition, my confusion turned into resentment. Dad began telling the media how he always supported me in my gymnastics career. The truth is that he didn't. It's so hard for me to write these words, because writing them forces me to face reality and not live in the protective bubble my mom tried to build around us when we were younger. After I finished the first night of trials, I received a text from my dad. "I need you to autograph some things for me 'cause I can't go back home empty handed." I was thinking, Why is it suddenly all about you? And where were you when I was struggling to get here? You haven't seen me in two years, and the first thing you want is my autograph? I cried the night after I read that text. Then after the final night at trials, Dad texted me again. "Brie, I took so many pictures with fans — lots and lots of small children who want to walk in your footsteps. I have so much to tell you about what God did. Everywhere I went God gave me honor and favor and congratulated me!" Never once did he simply say, "Congratulations."

Chapter Twenty-One

He gives us more grace.
—James 4:6, NIV

WEDNESDAY, JULY 18—THAT'S THE DAY THE FOUR OTHER MEMBERS of the US women's gymnastics team and I boarded a flight to London for the 2012 Summer Olympic Games.

"Are you excited?" Mom asked me that morning by phone. A couple weeks earlier, she'd flown to Iowa to see me before my departure to London, and after spending three days with me, she returned to Virginia Beach to prepare for her own trip to the Olympics.

"I am *soooo* excited!" I said.

"You can do this," Mom told me. "You have a chance to impact millions of people's lives. I believe in you, baby girl."

About a week earlier, on July 11, I flew from Iowa to Texas—the women's team first gathered at the Károlyi ranch for an Olympic preparation camp. Super early on the morning of my flight out of West Des Moines, Travis and Missy drove me to the airport; I'd given all my good-bye hugs to the girls at bedtime the night before, because I knew they'd be asleep when I left at five the following morning.

Just before we walked out of the house, Missy tucked a large envelope in my bag. In it, she'd gathered about twenty letters from all my friends and family—including my mother, siblings, grandmother, aunt, and of course her, Travis, and the girls. Each envelope had a date written on the front, signaling the day I was supposed to open it. The first letter was one from Missy. "These letters are from everyone who cares about you and is walking you through this journey," it read. "We all love you very much." I was already holding back tears, and I hadn't even opened all the letters!

Missy and Travis walked me as far into the airport terminal as they could. "We'll be praying for you," Travis said. Missy gave me the same advice she'd been offering me since my vault mistake at Pacific Rim. "Remember," she said, "you have two jobs. One is to always give one hundred percent, and the other is to listen to Coach Chow." I was ready to do both.

The overnight flight from Houston to London's Heathrow Airport felt long—nearly ten hours—but not nearly as long as that flight to Tokyo's World Championships had been. I alternated between watching a bit of a movie, napping, and catching up with McKayla, Kyla, Jordyn, and Aly about the adventure we'd all just begun.

"Can you believe we're actually on our way to London?" I said to Aly, who was sitting next to me.

"I know," she said, "It's completely surreal."

We'd all known each other for a while, of course; over the years, we'd seen each other at numerous camps and competitions. By the time the Olympics rolled around, we'd bonded enough to give our team a nickname—the Fierce Five. We originally called ourselves the Fab Five, but when we realized that name was already taken by a 1991 University of Michigan basketball team, McKayla and Jordan googled a bunch of other words that began with the letter *F*. The top two choices were *fierce* and *feisty*. Though there will always be plenty of feistiness to go around in our group, we agreed on *fierce* because we'd come prepared to go to battle toward one goal—a first-place finish for Team USA.

Speaking of first place, I'd already focused my gaze on a gold medal. Or two. Or more. As far back as I can recall, my mother has encouraged me to use visualization as a powerful tool, something I'd done when I shifted my perspective on the uneven bars. When I was living with the Partons, I hung a special prayer on a board next to my bed so that I could see it daily and meditate on those things I wanted to work toward in my life. Mom created a prayer for me, and she emailed it to me on October 10, 2010. We call it Our Secret (to success). For almost two years, I have prayed these words, and I have watched my faith grow, especially when times got really rough. This is the prayer:

- I can do all things through the anointing, which strengthens me.

- I am strong and I compete beautifully on vault, bars, beam, and floor.

- My routines are amazing because the Greater One lives on the inside of me.

- I refuse to give up! I refuse to quit! I push toward my dream, knowing that it will be my reality. I will achieve and be successful at everything I set my hand to do.

- I am a winner. I am a fierce competitor. I am a phenomenal gymnast.

- **Vault:** I complete my double and two-and-a-half vault with great power and precision. I stick each landing because I have the God-given talent and the intense desire to do it.

- **Bars:** I compete each element with great grace and strength. I will not fall, but instead my routine will flow beautifully. I stick each landing because the Greater One on the inside of me empowers me to.

- **Beam:** I compete each skill with grace and extreme power. I refuse to fall because I am more than a conqueror and Adonai loves me. I will excel and stick my dismounts because of the power that rests in and on me.

- **Floor:** I compete each element with perfect style and beauty. All of my dance elements are exquisite! All of my tumbling passes are executed with extreme precision. Every landing is perfect because God has equipped me with all that I need to succeed!

Once we arrived in London, there wasn't much time for sightseeing. But on our drive from the airport, I did catch a glimpse of the London Eye, that enormous Ferris wheel that rotates high above the city's skyline. When the wheel was first built back in 1999, it was the tallest one in the world; the tallest now is the Singapore Flyer. Later, during my stay in London, I squeezed in some time to ride the Ferris wheel and look out over the glittering lights of the city below, with the Thames River stretching and winding through it. Gorgeous!

Our first stop: the Olympic Village. That's the group of buildings with rooms to house the athletes. It features a humongous cafeteria that has every kind of cuisine you can imagine, 24/7: Mediterranean, Indian, American. The village is meant to be a haven away from the surrounding city and crowds, a place where not even press members are allowed. But that doesn't stop some wild things from happening in there: once inside, some of the most famous Olympians are mobbed by other athletes who want to get their signatures. The other girls and I went crazy when we spotted Michael Phelps. "Oh my gosh, can I take my photo with you?" I asked him. He kindly posed with me. And the whole time I was in the village, I was on the lookout for one of my favorite Olympians, Jamaican sprinter Usain Bolt. As it turns out, I never snapped his pic.

Each building in the village is assigned a country. The Chinese athletes' building, for instance, has its flags waving in front of a dormitory, as does the USA and dozens of other nations. In our team's part of the building, the rooms were set off in quads. So Márta Károlyi's room was at the entrance to our quad, and a set of stairs led up to two additional levels where our rooms were located. Jordyn and Aly shared a bedroom, Kyla and McKayla were roommates. And since there was an odd number of us on the team, I had a room of my own—the perfect place for me to sit, sing, pray, and focus before the greatest test of my life.

We'd all trained plenty hard before we arrived, of course—but do you think the training stopped when we got to London? Wrong! In fact, Chow was in rare form. He pushed me harder, faster, and higher than he did even back in West Des Moines. We worked out for five hours a day. But it was against regulation to train in the North Greenwich Arena, the site for our competition, so we went to a separate facility. A couple days before the real action, there's something called podium training, a kind of mini meet where gymnasts do their routines in front of judges in the actual arena. This gives everyone a chance to get used to the apparatuses, which may be a little different from the ones they've trained on. Even though the scores don't count at podium training, we still all try to make a good impression on the judges. I know I do.

When you're competing in an arena with thousands of

noisy people, you've gotta learn how to block out distractions—like screaming, name shouting ("Go, Gabby!"), whistling, and camera flashing. Sometimes when you first get to a meet, you're like, *Oh my gosh, everyone's cheering—what if I mess up?* That's where Chow's training comes in.

"Everybody gather around!" Chow would yell to get the attention of my other teammates in his gym. Once the gymnasts were standing around the apparatus, they shouted things like, "Yay, Gabby!" and "Way to go!" while I did my routine. It's Chow's way of mimicking the kinds of interruptions we will surely face at a major sporting event in an enormous arena. "Just shut out the crowd and focus on performing your skills," he'd tell me. "I want you to imagine that it's just you and this beam." Ten days after I set foot in London, I wouldn't have to imagine anymore. I'd be performing the real routine.

My mother and my siblings flew into London's Heathrow Airport on July 26. She, my sisters, and my brother stayed at a flat my mom rented. Thankfully, my family received some help from Olivia, my friend and teammate from Chow's gym who is from England: Olivia's father asked his good friends Mossie and Gillian to host Miss Carolyn and Tia, as well as Missy and Travis. (The hosts get to be hosted … funny, right?) Mom had raised money by designing T-shirts with my sister Joyelle (who is an amazing artist) and selling them online. Her yellow "Team Gabby" shirts featured the London Games. Did I mention that yellow is my favorite color?

I talked with my family frequently on Skype. "Proud of you, Brie!" Arie said. "Don't be afraid!" John added. "Stay strong!" Joy yelled out. Every day when the sun rose above our village and the hours drew closer to my big moment, the prayers, encouragement, support, and inspiration of my beloved family hovered above me. It felt like pure love. Even now, it still does.

Chapter Twenty-Two

What we are is God's gift to us.
What we become is our gift to God.
—ELEANOR POWELL

IT DIDN'T HIT ME UNTIL THE DAY I WALKED INTO NORTH GREENWICH Arena—*I am actually at the Olympics*. For a moment after the team arrived for podium training, I stood in silence at the edge of the room. Simultaneously widening my eyes and lifting my gaze upward, I scanned the room to take it all in: the hot-pink floor; the 16,500 seats, some so high up I could barely see them; the commentators, all busy setting up for their broadcasts. And the scent—for some reason, it smelled like a freezer to me. Crazy, right?

Six mornings later, on the very last day of July, I lingered in bed a bit longer than usual, imagining how the next twenty-four hours would unfold. On my dresser, one of Mom's letters—delivered by Missy in that thoughtful send-off package—still laid open.

"Breeeeeezy!" Mom had written. "You are an Olympian!

You did it! When you're preparing to compete, I want you to remember that you always end up on top. Never forget that God has made you the head, and not the tail." My long-sleeved red leo, so shiny and sparkly, was already at the foot of my bed in anticipation of the Fierce Five's big battle. This was it—the team competition.

A few days earlier, our Olympic games began rather dramatically. During the women's individual qualification round, I turned in the performance of my life. I nailed just about every one of my skills, from that tough Amanar vault to my final tumbling pass on floor. "Excellent job!" Chow said, embracing me at the sidelines afterward. My teammates also delivered top-notch routines, and with every flip and turn, Team USA put itself in a stronger position. By evening's end, in fact, three of the top four spots were filled by American gymnasts. Behind Russia's Viktoria Komova in first place, Aly qualified in second place with a score of 60.391. I came in third with 60.265. And Jordyn claimed fourth with 60.032. But because of a two-gymnast-per-country rule, Jordyn, the reigning world champion, wouldn't advance to the finals. The world was shocked. And as thrilled as both Aly and I were that we'd have the opportunity to compete for the all-around gold, we were also truly disappointed for our teammate. Yes, every gymnast on our team traveled to London to battle for that ultimate prize. Yet each one of us still came with a heart, one that broke when we saw our teammate weeping on the sidelines. Afterward, back at the village, we rallied around Jordyn and tried to lift her spirits. We also told her just how much we all needed her to regroup for our next fight.

On the night of team finals, our big job was to set aside every potential distraction and refocus on one goal — team victory. If we pulled it off, we'd be only the second US women's team to go golden since the Magnificent Seven did that for the first time at Atlanta's 1996 Olympics. I was the only gymnast slated to compete in all four apparatuses, and as the hour of my first exercise drew closer, a bunch of butterflies took flight in my stomach. I paced at the sidelines.

First up was Jordyn. She set the tone for our team's performance that evening by delivering an extraordinary vault exercise that earned her a score of 15.933. Later, when I took my position for vault, my mind flashed through all the training techniques Chow had given me. "Instead of running fast at first," he once told me, "start out slow, get your rhythm, and then speed up." I steadied myself on the floor and drew in a breath. *Run slowly … then faster … extend palms toward vault … square off the shoulders … pop off the table … soar high into the air with two and a half twists … and then … stick it!* An excellent beginning for me: 15.966 on vault.

As the evening inched on, every girl on our team turned in one dazzling routine after another. Our two biggest rivals in the competition, Romania and Russia, and another strong contender, China, all completed their rotations before we did. That meant that by the time we got to the final floor exercise, we knew exactly what we needed to score to go home with a gold. As we headed into the fourth and final event, here's how everything stacked up: USA at 138.230 (yay!). Russia at 136.931. China at 133.597. And Romania at 131.714.

Here's the thing: when you find yourself in the top spot — or maybe *especially* when you're temporarily number one — that's not the time to break out in a round of high fives. In this sport, the difference between a win and a loss often comes down to mere tenths of a point. So with one tiny slip or falter, what seems like a done deal can quickly come undone. So as ecstatic as we all were to see our position after the first three rounds, we knew we still needed to go out there and rock the house.

And boy did we. As each of the remaining countries took their turns, Aly, Jordyn, and I — USA's competitors on floor — all jogged on the sidelines to warm up. I was the first of the three to compete. Win or lose, I had already made a choice: I would have fun with this. I took a small extra step on my first tumbling pass (shoot!), but then I nailed all the others — and I stuck that landing before striking my final pose. Jordyn then proved her resilience and team spirit when she turned out a brilliant routine. Finally, Aly took the floor for the final performance of the evening. As the tune of the Hebrew folk song "Hava Nagila" piped up, Aly hit one tumbling pass after another and ended with a vibrant smile. The only thing left to do was wait and stare up at the scoreboard. No matter how well you think you've done, you're never certain of your position until those numbers actually appear. Had we pulled it off?

Long pause. And then at last, the scores: US with 183.596. Russia with 178.530. Romania with 176.414. We had done it!

"U-S-A!" the crowd chanted. "U-S-A!" The five of us huddled, wiped away buckets of tears, and hugged for what seemed like a lifetime—which is pretty close to what each of us had spent to get to that arena.

"Can you believe it?" I said to McKayla.

"It's so amazing!" she screamed.

That night, back in the village, we laughed, hugged, recounted the best moments of the night—but we knew we had to save the real party for much later. This girl needed her rest! Especially when, in less than forty-eight hours, I'd face the greatest test of my entire gymnastics career.

The all-around women's gymnastics competition is the pinnacle event in my sport. Mary Lou Retton, the first US gymnast to ever claim the prize, went golden back in 1984 at the Los Angeles games. Only two other American gymnasts followed: Carly Patterson in the 2004 Athens Olympics and Nastia Liukin in Beijing's 2008 games. As you already know, since I was eight, I've dreamed of becoming the fourth on that list. On a Thursday evening in London, I got my golden opportunity.

That morning, I reached into my suitcase and pulled out the day's letter—another one from Mom, the third I'd received in the batch. In it, my mother offered exactly the kind of encouragement I needed. Here is a portion of Mom's letter:

Hey, Baby Girl,

As you go to strive for the next part of making your dream come true, just remember that you have worked very hard for this moment! Be strong in the Lord and in the power of His might. Joshua comes to mind as I think about you today. God told Moses to go take the land from the people who were occupying the Promised Land (Joshua 1:9 – 11): "Haven't I ordered you, 'Be strong, be bold'? So don't be afraid or downhearted, because Adonai your God is with you wherever you go." Y'hoshua instructed the officials of the people to go through the camp and order the people, "Prepare provisions, because in three days you will cross this Yarden to go in and take possession of the land Adonai your God is giving you."

Gabrielle, you have seen many miracles that God has done. You have experienced the glory and anointing of God. May the Blessing of the Most High God overtake you and cause everything you set your hand to do to prosper!

By the way, did you know that it rained on Monday? Of course, I thought about the anointing, and I thought about you. No need to doubt or worry or fear. You can stand strong knowing that the Lord our God is with you. He will never leave you or forsake you. Continue to rejoice, my love! Time to go take possession of what God is giving to you. Be strong. Be courageous. Be confident. Go walk into your Promised Land.

All my love,
Ma

For years, my mother has told me that rain is God's way of showering down His anointing and good favor on us. "Look, Mom," I said back during the American Cup. "It's raining." We both instantly knew what that meant: God is here, and He's about to show out! So when I spotted London's rain on the morning of the all-around, it felt like a forecast of what the day may hold.

I Skyped my mother that morning with a note: "Mom, you think I can do this?"

"I absolutely know you can, sweetheart," she answered without hesitation.

Later that day, my brother gave me his final pep talk: "Remember our motto, Brie," he said. "In order to be the best, you've got to take out the best."

Before I left my room in the village, I quoted my favorite verse: "I can do all things through Christ who strengthens me." I felt ready.

I put my hair up in a ponytail, the same type most gymnasts wear, and then I pulled back some stray strands using clips. And speaking of my hair—I'm sure you've heard that it suddenly became a big topic on Twitter after the team finals. Some people commented that they didn't think my hairstyle was neat. Other comments are too ridiculous to even repeat. When I heard about the tweets,

I thought, *I'm competing for the top prize in an elite sport, and you're talking about my hairstyle?* Though it did sting at first, I made a choice: I couldn't let that distract me. I'd worked too hard to get to this place. I refused to waste even a second on negativity. Later, some of the rude tweeters thankfully apologized—and I still accept, lol. Hundreds of others followed up on Facebook and Twitter to express their support. They understood what I did: This moment wasn't about the hair on my head. It was about the courage in my heart.

On the evening of the individual all-around competition, each of my teammates embraced me before I took the floor wearing a jewel-lined fuchsia leo nearly as bright as the arena floor. "Good luck," Aly and I said to each other at the sidelines. I then started my warm up for the first event, the vault. I glanced up into the stands and saw Mom waving and cheering like crazy as I took my starting position. *This was it.*

I raised my arms and saluted the judges. Then just like Chow had taught me, I ran slowly up the track before exploding into a sprint, and—*pop!*—the exercise that I've spent hundreds of hours perfecting was over in an instant. I nearly stepped off the track during my landing on the first vault, but I still earned a spectacular starting score: 15.966. *Phew!*

Next up was bars—the apparatus I'd once loathed, which is why it's ironic it has become my signature event. As I chalked my hands in preparation for the exercise, I recalled what Chow once told me: "A great bar routine is like a beautiful song—it should have a nice rhythm and flow." So with every turn, kip, giant, and the landing I stuck (yes!), I focused on creating an unforgettable melody—a routine that was as technically awesome as it was inspirational. The crowd applauded my every flip. Onlookers yelled out "Go, Gabby!" But just as we'd practiced, I kept my concentration. And as it turns out, Chow's approach was the right one: I widened my lead over Russia's Viktoria Komova. Whoa. That lead even held up after I completed my tricky beam routine—one I pulled off without a single major mistake, I might add. "Thank you, God," I whispered after I'd flipped off that four-inch beam. His rain was pouring down.

By the time I went into my last rotation of the evening, the floor exercise, I was only in the lead by .3126—a score I knew could easily be overtaken. Talk about a nail biter!

The announcer came over the loudspeaker: "On the floor, representing the United States of America— Gabrielle Douglas!" I put my body in position right at the corner of the floor. Just then, the first notes of my song, "We Speak No Americano," blared from the speakers; I chose that upbeat number because I knew it would rev up the crowd. As I took my first tumbling pass, the arena exploded with cheers. *Yes, I nailed the first landing!* The crowd clapped along. I did step out of bounds once, but the next two series of flips were clean. *Oh my goodness, I'm actually doing this!* Before I took my last tumble, I drew in a breath. *Okay—here I go.* I then hurled my body into the air, and with every bit of effort I could muster, I tried to stick that final landing. *Done*! Whatever happened next, I knew I'd done my best. After the score was posted—a 15.033—all I could do was wait.

Viktoria Komova was the last to take her turn on the floor that evening. And the whole time I watched her routine from the sidelines, my head was spinning. *Will Viktoria make a comeback? Will my score hold up? Could I actually go home with a gold?* From start to finish, an entire floor routine is one minute and thirty seconds. It seemed like I waited for an eternity for my score to flash, especially when I witnessed what everyone else did: Viktoria's exercise was fantastic.

The arena went silent as we awaited the result. My eyes were fixed on the scoreboard. I looked up. And I waited. And I waited. Finally, there it was. The final results of the all-around scores: Gabrielle Douglas, 62.232, Viktoria Komova, 15.100. I was in the top spot. And that was the moment that my life changed forever.

I was so overwhelmed with joy that I could hardly think or speak! So instead, I leapt—right into the arms of my coach. "Thank you, Chow," I said. We both cried as we embraced.

That night, I made three kinds of history: I became the first African American and the first woman of color of any nationality to ever win a gold medal in the individual all-around competition. I became the fourth American female gymnast to win the gold. And I became the first US gymnast to ever receive both the team gold medal and the individual all-around gold medal in a single Olympic games. I had done it. On a rainy Thursday afternoon in London, my God had made it all possible. And of course, I couldn't have done it without my family, my coaches, and my host family being right there by my side the entire time.

During the medal ceremony, an official placed the wide, purple ribbon holding my gold medal around my neck. I held on tightly to the flower arrangement I'd been handed. The gold felt so much heavier than I'd imagined!

Up on the podium, the announcer came over the loud-speaker: "Please stand for the national anthem of the United States of America." My country's flag raised into the air. As the familiar tune began, my hands trembled a bit as a new set of tears formed in the corners of my eyes. I took a deep breath and looked all around the arena. The whole time, I was thinking, *Am I dreaming?*

As I stood before thousands, and millions more watched from every corner of the globe, a series of memories reeled through my head: My first day at Gymstrada a decade before. The hundreds of double shifts Mom had worked to cover my fees. The countless hours I'd spent in training. The difficult two-year separation from my family. That day seven months earlier when I almost gave up on my goal. In an instant, all the sacrifices, the injuries, and the homesickness felt worth it. On August 2, 2012, my leap of faith became God's gracious gift to me.

"Oh, say does that star-spangled banner yet wave," played the final part of the anthem. "O'er the land of the free ... and the home ... of the ... brave!" The crowd erupted into the loudest cheer I may hear in this lifetime. I suddenly felt like the star of a rock concert! The other medalists congratulated me. Camera flashes lit up in every corner of the arena. My family and friends cried into each other's arms. And for as long as I am alive, I will always remember that moment. I give God all of the glory, and that's a win-win situation. The glory goes up to Him, and the blessings fall down on me.

The Resting Place

Everyone makes mistakes. For most of my childhood, that's what I've told myself whenever I've thought about my father. I've wanted to forgive him and start fresh. My sister Joyelle, my brother, John, and I have all tried to look beyond the countless gymnastic and track meets, football games, and other events that our dad chose to miss while we were growing up. I've always adored my father—and that's why I've felt so torn. I've struggled to reconcile my love for Dad with the fact that he wasn't around and didn't contribute as much as he should have financially. Yes, there were times when he was overseas. But where was he during all those years when he was right there in my city? I wanted him to be in my life. That's why it hurt so much when he wasn't. I was dealing with all of these difficult feelings even as I worked toward my Olympic dream.

In my heart, I've always carried a secret hope that my dad would change—that he would suddenly become the father that I craved. And while maybe one day he will, I've chosen to free myself by accepting the way things are for now. Why not forever? Because there has to be room for grace. Not just for my dad, but for all of us.

Some would call me the child of an absent father. I call myself the child of the King. Because while my earthly dad sometimes didn't come through for me, my heavenly Father always will. He answered Mom's prayers when our family fought to stay warm in the back of that Dodge van. He has carried me through disease, heartache, injury, and isolation. He is my great provider. And it is in His amazing arms that I now rest.

Afterword

I'M A WILD SLEEPER. SO AFTER I WON THOSE TWO GOLD MEDALS IN London, I didn't stash them under my pillow. I instead put them right beside my bed on a tabletop. I couldn't risk twitching during the night and then having the medals slip, fall, and break. I would never forgive myself!

Practically before my last medal ceremony was over, tweets came pouring in from all kinds of famous people. Lil' Wayne tweeted, "Glad I lived to see what Gabby Douglas did in the Olympics. Icon." I received "flowing happy tears" from Oprah (WOW). I also got congrats from the cast of my favorite TV show, *The Vampire Diaries*, as well as from Beyoncé, Nikki Minaj, Gabrielle Union, Octavia Spencer, Elizabeth Banks, Holly Robinson Peete, Whoopi Goldberg, and so many others. (Thanks, everyone!) I even got a tweet from a fellow Olympian: "Congrats to @gabrielledoug last night! We watched from the pool!!!" Michael Phelps wrote.

It's weird to be suddenly famous. All those years when I'd been dreaming about winning a gold, I hadn't thought too much about how my life would change if I actually *won.* I thought I could just fly to London, win a medal, and then simply fly back home to Virginia Beach and hang out with my family. Well, that's not quite the way it turned out! If I'm simply walking down the street, people are like, "Look, there's Gabby!" As much fun as that is, I don't think I'll ever get used to everyone recognizing me. Now I'm a little nervous about going out in flip-flops and wearing no makeup. I'm thinking, *What if the paparazzi take my photo when I look crazy?*

On those days when I just want to be a regular teen-ager again (whatever that is!), I wear my disguise, which is shades and a hat. It hardly ever works, lol! Once, when I was in the grocery store in Virginia Beach with Mom and John, a guy went, "Hey—there's that gymnast!" Another time, I was strolling down Rodeo Drive in Los Angeles, a man actually stopped traffic by hopping out of his car just so he could run over and take a picture with me. The other drivers were beeping their horns like crazy.

Eight days after my victory in the individual all-around competition (and by the way, it *still* feels like a dream!), Mom and I took a direct flight from London to Los Angeles so I could be a guest on *The Jay Leno Show.* My first thought was, *What in the world am I going to wear?* Before I left London, I sent all of my clothes home to Virginia Beach with my sister Arielle—I didn't want to lug around all that stuff with me. So with Jay Leno and so many other appearances coming up, like ringing the opening bell at the New York Stock Exchange and going on *Letterman*, I didn't have a stitch of clothing with me.

What I did have was one full day to shop—and a mother who was right there beside me to help out. Mom and I went to the BCBG store on Rodeo Drive. "How about this?" Mom said as she held up a gold skirt and the cutest black jacket. "I love it!" I said. After Mom picked out a couple of other show-stopping outfits for me, I was ready for lights, camera, action!

A couple days later, on August 12, I appeared with the First Lady, Michelle Obama, on *The Jay Leno Show*. When I first saw her, I thought, *She is so tall!* Mrs. Obama and I chatted for a moment after the taping, and she was funny, down to earth, and cool.

"Congratulations!" she said to me. "I'm so proud of you."

"Well, thank you!" I said.

"Let me know if you need anything," she said.

"Well," I joked, "maybe I can have a sleepover with your girls at the White House."

She chuckled. "Yes, definitely. I think that's a great idea."

Fingers crossed that I'll one day get to meet Sasha, Malia, and even the president! And speaking of President Obama, did I mention he called me and my teammates after Team USA won gold? "Congratulations," he said. "I'm proud of you." What an honor it was to talk with him!

A few days after Jay Leno's show, I flew to New York to cohost *America's Got Talent* with Nick Cannon. When I put my double gold medals on backstage, Nick Cannon joked, "Hey, Two Chains!" (As in 2 Chainz, the rapper

... hilarious!). A moment later, Nick introduced me to a roaring crowd as the show's judges all gave me a standing ovation. Can you say *goose bumps*?

An absolute whirlwind—that's how I'd describe the months that have followed the Olympic Games. I've had my picture featured on a Kellogg's Corn Flakes cereal box (cheese!); bumped around on a bus across the country for the Kellogg's Tour of Gymnastics (so awesome to reunite with the Fierce Five); met Oprah for an interview at the Partons' house (my first trip back to Des Moines ... what a sweet reunion!); got all glammed up to be on the cover of *Essence*; threw out a pitch for the Mets at Citi Field in Los Angeles; met Pink and the (very!) McDreamy Patrick Dempsey on the season premiere of *The Ellen Degeneres Show*; led the pledge of allegiance at the Democratic National Convention (and the whole time backstage beforehand, I was thinking, *Oh no—what if I forget the words?* I did fine.); supported and worked the phone banks for the Stand Up for Cancer benefit (where I met stars like Gwyneth Paltrow, Tim McGraw, Mac Miller, fellow Olympian Missy Franklin, Julia Roberts, Donald Faison, Minka Kelly, Kobe Bryant, and so many others who all came together to raise money for cancer research); encouraged drivers to stop texting while driving (because seriously, folks, it can wait ...); starred in a video-game commercial (love my Nintendo 3DS!); and signed more autographs than I ever thought possible. As much of a mouthful all of that was, it's not even the end of the list!

A couple of my experiences were so amazing that I want to give you some of the details. So here goes.

On September 6, 2012, my teammates and I appeared on the MTV Video Music Awards—aka "The VMAs." On the night of the event, a team of hair and makeup artists went to work on me and Mom in the hotel; someone was even painting our fingernails and toes! The makeup artist asked me, "Okay, what do you like?" I said, "I love foundation, blush, eye shadow, mascara, lip balm—all the good stuff!" When I'm competing, I prefer a natural look—but for special occasions, I go all out! Once the hairstylist gave me some long, loose, and flowing layers that worked perfectly with my outfit—a shimmery gold-and-black sequined dress, black heeled booties, and dangly earrings—I couldn't wait to walk the red carpet.

The girls and I pulled up to the event inside a car with tinted windows. "Roll down your windows! Roll down your windows!" chanted a big group of fans who had gathered. Since there were so many Escalades and Cadillacs rolling around, the crowd didn't know who was in which car—but they figured we must be famous, so they screamed. When my teammates and I finally stepped out of the car, they began another chant: "U-S-A! U-S-A!" We walked onto the red carpet right behind Miley Cyrus, and that was such an awesome feeling! Everyone was taking pictures of her and screaming, "Look this way, Miley!" Then a guy screamed out, "Gabby, can we get your picture?" Dozens of other photos followed.

The whole night, I was surrounded by all of my favorite stars. When Katy Perry spotted me, she said, "Gabby, I love you!" She came running up to me, grabbed a camera, and snapped a picture of us. Later, I got to sit in the front row and shake hands with Chris Brown, who's from Virginia. I also met Rihanna, Taylor Swift, and, of course, Alicia Keys—my partner on stage. I got to perform with her and Nicki Minaj that night.

Before my number, I practiced the flips I was supposed to do as Alicia sang "Girl on Fire." Alicia and Nicki couldn't be there for my trial run, so I just rehearsed on my own by going through all of the tumbles once. Then right before our appearance, I did the fastest clothing change I've ever done: in twenty-five seconds, I swapped my dress for a pair of leather leggings and a flowing, sparkly top. Trying to make it out there on time was totally nerve-wracking. Right after my teammates and I were onstage announcing Alicia Keys's entrance, I rushed backstage to change. I was back there trying to tug those skinny leather pants up my legs—but they were sticking to my skin! I got them on just in time to go out there. The handsprings were fine. My shirt was not. As I was bounding through the air, the top flew right up into my face! Thankfully, the crowd didn't see much except for my bra straps. The whole evening was unforgettable. I felt like I'd leapt right off that London podium and right into a Hollywood dream.

Later in September, I had an experience that still gives me chills whenever I think about it: I visited the set of my all-time favorite TV series, *The Vampire Diaries*. My day there was even more special because my sister Joyelle, who has watched every episode of that show with me, got to come along with Mom and me.

Why do we love the series so much? Because you never quite know what'll happen next ... it's always unexpected. Way back when we first saw a preview of *The Vampire Diaries*, Joy and I weren't so sure we'd tune in—we're hardcore Twilight fans and we thought we'd just stick with that. But one night when we were clicking through the channels, we started watching *The Vampire Diaries*, and we've been hooked ever since.

I was beside myself with excitement when the show's producers arranged for me to appear in a scene on their set in Atlanta. Do you notice me trembling a bit because I got to meet Ian Somerhalder? He plays Damon on the show, and I've had the hugest crush on that guy forever. Actually, all the cast members are pretty hot—I met them all that day. After I'd filmed my two scenes (who knew actors had to do so many takes?), Mom, Joy, and I went on a backstage tour of the set. That place is enormous!

Can you believe I've done all of this before I even have my driver's license? And yes, I'm planning to get that real soon. In Iowa, Travis took me out in his truck a few times and taught me some basics; we didn't get too far, though, because I was scared I was going to hit a deer—there are so many of them there. And now that the Olympics are over, I'm back in homeschool and finishing off my high-school diploma. I eventually want to go to acting school.

Ever since I did that cameo on *Vampire Diaries* (so what if it was a nonspeaking part?), I have been bitten by the acting bug! Hard to believe that I'm the same girl who was once so shy that I clutched my mother's leg! What a difference two golds make.

What's next for me? For one thing, I can't wait to catch my breath and simply chillax with Mom, Arie, Joy, and John. Secondly, I'll eventually start training again. That's right, I've already started dreaming about my next leap of faith, the 2016 Rio Olympics. "You haven't even reached your peak," my coach keeps telling me. I know that means he's planning to push me harder than he ever has—and I'm ready. Bring it on, Chow!

Grace. Gold. Glory. Those three little words now have the biggest meaning for me. Grace—that's all about how my Father's love, mercy, and forgiveness will never (ever) run out. Gold—yes, that describes the pair of medals I will always feel so privileged to wear, but it's also the standard we can use in how kindly we treat one another. Glory—when God shares it with us, there's only one thing we can do: give it right back to Him.

Acknowledgments

So many awesome people have believed in me and supported me during my journey. To all those who've offered me your love, encouragement, prayers, and hugs, I appreciate you. Here are a few I'd like to honor publicly:

My sports agent, Sheryl Shade: Thanks for everything you've done for me and my career, and managing everything so I can focus on competing.

My literary agent, Frank Weimann: Thank you for handling the publishing side of my career and helping to make me an author.

My cowriter, Michelle Burford: I enjoyed spending time with you and am so proud of the book we worked on together!

My coaches, Liang Chow and Liwen Zhuang, who I affectionately call Chow and Li: Thank you for helping me believe in the talent God blessed me with, and for giving me the training I needed to tap into my potential as an elite athlete.

My grandparents, Granddad and Miss Carolyn: Thank you for coming to my competitions and helping out when my family needed it most.

My Tia, Bianca: You've always been there with exactly the encouragement I needed.

My host parents, Travis and Missy Parton: Thank you for opening your home, welcoming me in, and loving me as one of your own.

My host sisters, Hailey, Lexi, Leah, and Elissa: You shared your mom and dad with me and kept me laughing constantly!

Pastor Quintin Stieff: I appreciate all of the spiritual lessons and prayers.

Jim and Susan Mars, Bill and Vicki Parton, Dustin and Ann Mars, Matt and Amanda Oleson: I'm grateful that you stepped in and became my family while I was away from home.

My Chow's Gym family: Thank you for always cheering for me!

And of course none of this could have been accomplished without the skills of my team at Zondervan, a division of HarperCollins. Thanks to the captain of my book team, Lisa Sharkey, who signed me up, and to Jacque Alberta, who has worked around the clock to get the manuscript in shape. Much appreciation also goes to Art Director Cindy Davis, Photo Editor Kim Tanner, the marketing team of Chriscynethia Floyd, Sara Merritt, and Jonathan Michael, the Composition team of Ben Fetterley and Greg Johnson, and the incredible sales force at Zondervan. My gratitude also goes to HarperCollins CEO Brian Murray, HarperCollins Christian Division CEO Mark Schoenwald, and SVP and Publisher Annette Bourland for your enthusiasm and support for this project.

Discussion Questions

1. Just seven months before the Olympics, Gabrielle wanted to quit gymnastics. Have you ever felt like quitting even after you put in lots of hard work, persistence, and hope? What made you want to quit? How do you continue on and not give up?

2. Is there a parent, sibling, or family member whom you wish was in your life more consistently? Who do you talk to about these feelings? How can you stay positive toward that person?

3. Gabrielle's mom prayed for God to heal her daughter over and over, and he did. Have you witnessed an answer to prayer like that? Do you believe God hears all of your prayers even if he doesn't answer the way you ask him to?

4. Gabrielle reflects on some fun memories from her childhood throughout the book. What family traditions or childhood memories have shaped your life?

5. Sometimes people don't realize how upsetting their words can be. Have you ever teased someone and found out later their feelings were hurt? Or have you ever said something about a person's appearance or personality? How can you make things right with that person?

6. Gabrielle knew she wanted to go to the Olympics when she saw Carly Patterson win the all-around

gold at the 2004 Summer Games. Has someone inspired you to do something big? Who is it, and how has their accomplishment motivated you?

7. Moving to Iowa was a big step for Gabrielle, from leaving her family to starting with a new coach and a new training regimen. But it was one she felt she needed to take. Have you ever made a decision you felt was necessary? How did that leap of faith turn out?

8. Being a good winner or a good loser says a lot about a person's character. What did you notice about Gabrielle's treatment of her teammates when they beat her? How about when she beat them?

9. Gabrielle's family and host family played an important role in her gymnastics success and in keeping her grounded. How do you support your friends and family members in their goals and struggles? How do your friends and family encourage and guide your life?

10. Gabrielle's mom always reminds her of God's promises. What Scriptures (or quotes) do you know that bring comfort, peace, or strength? What verses included in this book remind you of something important?

Talk It Up!

Want free books?
First looks at the best new fiction?
Awesome exclusive merchandise?

We want to hear from you!

Give us your opinions on titles, covers, and stories.
Join the Z Street Team.

Visit zstreetteam.zondervan.com/joinnow
to sign up today!

Also—Friend us on Facebook!

www.facebook.com/goodteenreads

- Video Trailers
- Connect with your favorite authors
- Sneak peeks at new releases
- Giveaways
- Fun discussions
- And much more!